RELATIONSHIPS, ASTROLOGY AND KARMA

RELATIONSHIPS, ASTROLOGY AND KARMA

*How to Understand, Transform and Heal Your
Relationships Through Astrology*

PAULINE STONE

Aquarian/Thorsons
An Imprint of HarperCollins*Publishers*

The Aquarian Press
An Imprint of HarperCollins*Publishers*
77–85 Fulham Palace Road,
Hammersmith, London W6 8JB

Published by The Aquarian Press 1991
3 5 7 9 10 8 6 4 2

A catalogue record for this book
is available from the British Library

ISBN 0 85030 847 X

Typeset by Harper Phototypesetters Limited,
Northampton, England
Printed in Great Britain by
Mackays of Chatham, Kent

DEDICATION

To my darling BR without whose Capricorn support and commitment this book would not have been created.

ACKNOWLEDGEMENT

I wish to acknowledge all the clients and friends who gave permission for their stories to be recounted in adapted form in this book.

CONTENTS

AUTHOR'S NOTE

In this book my use of 'he' for the outer planet player and 'she' for the person whose inner planet is aspected by the outer planet reflects the relatively active role of the outer planet and the relatively passive role of the inner planet in a mutual aspect.

INTRODUCTION

Did you ever have the feeling, when introduced to someone for the first time, that they seemed familiar to you, that you had possibly known them before, some time, some place? This sense of 'déja vu' is experienced by many of us when we meet with individuals who are to play a major role in our life. In some cases the sense of familiarity is based merely on the stranger's resemblance to someone close to us whom we knew earlier in this life. But more often than not we are actually recognizing an individual with whom we have indeed had an important relationship—not in this life, but in a previous one.

Mostly there is no such thing as a 'new' relationship. In accordance with the universal law of karma, we meet repeatedly with the same souls, lifetime after lifetime, in order to work on the spiritual lessons for which we have incarnated. In one lifetime we may find ourselves in a parent/child relationship with a certain soul, in another lifetime we may form a husband/wife relationship with them. But in each case our purpose is the same—to work on interpersonal difficulties and try to get on better with each other.

Earth is the laboratory of our solar system, where we attempt to put into practice the spiritual theories symbolized by the planets. The challenge of life on earth is to learn to love and it is primarily through relationships that this is achieved—it is impossible to express love unless we have someone to share it with.

World peace is dependent upon peaceful relationships, not only at the international level but right down to the interpersonal level. Indeed, there can be no global harmony until each individual has achieved harmony with his or her own small world, and we can each play our part in improving world relations by transforming our personal relationships.

Our greatest obstacle to happy, fulfilling relationships is a basic lack of perception. Failure to understand why we habitually react in a negative way to a certain individual and they to us denies us the opportunity to change our behaviour patterns. Lack of awareness of the core issues which lie at the root of a host of minor interpersonal conflicts prevents us from tackling our relationship problems at their source.

Astrology provides a means of casting light on the dynamics of human relationships. It allows us to look objectively at ourselves and others, free of the confusing projections which normally cloud our judgement. By comparing our birth chart with that of another person we can pin-point the key issues around which our relationship with them is likely to revolve. We can also gain a fascinating insight into the karmic patterns we have formed with them over a number of previous incarnations.

Correct understanding of the karmic challenges which colour our contacts with one another lifetime after lifetime is a vital part of the process of healing our personal relationships. In order to transform our relationships we need to view them not simply from the standpoint of the here-and-now, but within a much wider context which encompasses the sum total of our associations with the other person, often spanning many thousands of years. Analysis of the cross-aspects between one person's chart and another's can give us this wider perspective.

In karmic astrology, cross-aspects between two charts symbolize the karmic account between the two individuals as it stands in this lifetime. As in the natal horoscope, flowing aspects such as the trine and sextile are representative of harmonious patterns, whilst hard aspects such as the square and opposition, as well as the conjunction, suggest that inharmonious and often negative modes of behaviour have been established. By paying special attention to the hard cross-aspects in a chart comparison, we uncover the hidden conflicts whose roots lie far back in time and which tie us to one another *ad infinitum* by a process of karmic bondage. Not until we have recognized, accepted and healed these conflicts can we release ourselves from our links with another soul. It is relatively easy to sever our physical ties with one another in the material world, but spiritual ties cannot be broken so readily.

The outer planets in a chart comparison symbolize the main learning areas in personal relationships. Thus Saturn, Uranus, Neptune and Pluto are each representative of a specific challenge likely to arise as we attempt to live out our lives alongside one another. The positive polarities of these planets stand for various aspects of unselfish love—our ultimate goal and the only means whereby we can finally free ourselves from karmic bondage. In contrast, the negative polarities of the outer planets symbolize the self-centred behaviour patterns which are the antithesis of love and which underlie the pain we often inflict on one another in our relationships.

Our challenge, especially now as the New Age comes into being, is to tap into the positive, loving polarities of the outer planets and to manifest these in our personal interactions. When we express the positive, loving polarity of a planet, as a karmic reaction we draw towards us positive, loving energy in the form of fulfilling, joyful relationships. But when we express only the negative, unloving polarity of a planet, we attract the same negative, unloving energy towards ourselves. By virtue of the law of cause and effect, in due course we will experience precisely the same pain that we ourselves have caused to others.

In order to maximize our potential to enjoy relationships of the highest quality, we need to look carefully at our ability—or lack of ability—to give and receive love. In our natal chart hard aspects of the outer planets to our Moon and Venus suggest the general difficulties we are likely to experience in any intimate relationship in terms of our habitual response to or expression of love. Within this framework, a comparison of our own chart with that of another person will focus on the precise nature of the challenge which this particular association will present. We now build up a detailed picture of how this relationship will test us in terms of the fundamental weaknesses shown in our natal chart. By consciously attempting to attune ourselves to the positive energies of the planets highlighted by the comparison, we heighten our capacity to give and receive love and thus to bring more joy into our own and others' lives.

Karma is not something we undergo simply as punishment in

retribution for our sins. The law of cause and effect operates in order that we may grow in understanding, for it is only by ourselves experiencing the very same suffering that our behaviour has inflicted on others, that we can appreciate the undesirability of that behaviour. In the process of learning which continuously unfolds within human relationships we all serve as one another's teachers—we are all the instruments of each other's karma.

Mostly, however, we are slow learners and we tend to repeat the same lessons lifetime after lifetime, forever re-enacting the same karmic scenarios with the same individuals. Ignorance of the karmic process and lack of insight into our own specific karmic predicament render us powerless to release ourselves from the patterns to which we are tied.

It is relatively easy to recognize a relationship likely to be of major karmic significance. There is always a strong feeling of familiarity accompanied either by a sense of easefulness and harmony when the past association has been a happy one, or by an inexplicable tension and mistrust when the past contact has been more problematic. Curiously, the strength of the mutual attraction may well be greater in the case of a difficult rather than an easy past-life relationship, as fear and hatred are the most powerful magnets in drawing souls to one another, presumably in order that they may complete their unfinished business.

Certainly, despite the mutual pull, the first meeting of two people with challenging karmic links is likely to be marked by a good deal of subconscious fear on both sides. Depending upon the planet most prominent in the chart comparison, their anxiety will centre around a particular interpersonal issue, such as control, responsibility or honesty, which lay at the source of their past-life conflicts. Somewhere in our far-memory we have perfect recall of our past-life relationships but normally all that will surface into our conscious mind is an ill-defined gut reaction to the other person and a hazy premonition of the likely outcome of the association.

Mutual defensiveness is also a salient feature of any 'new' relationship which has difficult karmic undertones. Our normal response to a sense of fear and insecurity is to seek to protect ourselves, and each party will tend to erect their own defensive barriers in accordance with the nature of the planets involved.

But if the relationship is destined to be of major significance in our life, sooner or later we will feel compelled to lower those defensive barriers. If, prior to incarnation, we have chosen to confront a particular individual in this lifetime, we will find ourselves powerless to prevent the process from unfolding—and invariably with all the old anger and grief.

What we can control, however, is our present reaction to these age-old emotions and to the person whom we believe to be causing us to experience them. It rests within our own hands as to whether we choose to re-enact yet again the same old karmic tragedy, or whether we have the courage to learn some new lines and make a fresh start in the relationship.

The ability to transform negative karmic relationship patterns is dependent on just one prerequisite: a willingness to refrain from retaliation. Of course, our instinctive reaction towards someone who causes us pain is to strike back along similar lines through a desire for vengeance. But if we accept that whatever unhappiness we suffer in life at the hands of others is always of our own making and that whatever hurt we inflict on others will eventually return to us, we must recognize that further negative behaviour on our part is only likely to cause us more pain in the long run. So that although in the short term we may gain the satisfaction of paying back our assailant, in the long term we are also wounding ourselves.

To spare ourselves future suffering, the most useful reaction to another's mistreatment of us is to stand back objectively and take a long cool look at ourselves. The fact is that we are only ever confronted with and strongly affected by a negative trait in another person, when that trait is powerful but unrecognized in our own psyche. Thus if we are able to perceive within ourselves the same kind of behaviour which we are condemning in someone else, we are taking the first step towards freeing ourselves of the need to meet with this behaviour at the hands of others. We are acknowledging the process of cause and effect and are thus initiating our release from our hard karma.

A chart comparison is invaluable in allowing us to pin-point the specific planetary energy which is resulting in painful karmic repercussions within a relationship and which we need to look at very carefully in ourselves. By endeavouring to transmute our own expression of that planet and draw only on its positive vibrations, we radiate love to the other person, perhaps in the form of for-giveness, perhaps in the form of letting go, depending upon the planet in question.

It is this expression of love along the lines of a specific outer planet which is the key to release from karmic bondage. In manifesting the positive qualities of the planet we obviate the need for further 'lessons' and will now attract only joyful karmic experiences in this area. Furthermore, our loving acceptance of the other person in the relationship is sufficiently powerful to dissolve any fear or hatred that they may still feel towards us. Thus it is unnecessary for both individuals in a relationship to change in order that their karmic link may be severed; it is enough for one alone to take the initiative.

The alternative to the non-retaliatory response is actually a grim option. In expressing aggression towards the other person, whether in a physical sense or in an equally powerful emotional sense, we simply condemn ourselves to further tedious suffering of the same ilk. And, perhaps most horrifyingly, we bond ourselves inseparably to our 'adversary' and guarantee ourselves at least one more future-life association. The embittered termination of a relationship, as in the case of some divorces, is never the longed-for final ending, rather just the beginning!

The forgiving approach is much easier once we have come to terms with our relationship with our parents and pardoned them for their mistakes towards us. Indeed, it is probably impossible to deal lovingly with people who cause us pain later in life unless we have first been able to let go of the pain inflicted on us by our parents.

The karma we undergo at the hands of our mother and father is of vital importance since it forms the root karma upon which all our future relationships in this lifetime will be based. The soul, in its wisdom, chooses to learn its major karmic lessons in childhood when our defences are lowest and we are at our most vulnerable. The pain which we suffer as children is the cruellest and the most difficult to eradicate, but until we are able to acknowledge and transmute the difficulties in our relationship with our parents we have little prospect of making a success of our adult relationships.

Whilst parental conflicts remain unresolved, our tendency may be unwittingly to attract towards us male or female figures who embody the same destructive traits as our mother or father. Or in other cases we may project such traits onto our partners or our children, although in reality they bear no resemblance whatsoever to our parents. In this way we can remain dogged throughout our lives by our childhood karmic experiences which effectively prevent us from enjoying adult associations for their true worth.

It is probably true to say that our relationships with our parents represent the central karmic theme for our present lifetime, of which all future relationships are simply reflections, enacted with individuals with whom we also possess karmic links. For this reason it is invaluable to conduct a detailed comparison of our parents' charts and our own in order to determine the key challenges likely to occur in all the major interpersonal contacts of our life.

THE ROLES OF THE OUTER PLANETS IN INTERPERSONAL RELATIONSHIPS

When we are cast in the role of an outer planet in a cross-aspect with another individual, we assume centre-stage. The spotlight falls upon us as the leading player in the real-life drama which we are destined to enact within the framework of the relationship, and the course of the drama rests essentially in our hands. The majority of the script will be written by us, and we have free choice in deciding upon the outcome of the final act. We are faced with an awesome responsibility of which we are rarely consciously aware.

When we meet with an individual who stimulates the expression of an outer planet in our chart, we are challenged by them to express the principle of that planet at the highest level of which we are capable. However, especially where hard cross-aspects are involved, the individual may initially elicit the lowest vibrations of the respective planetary energy.

Frequently something in the way we perceive the other person stimulates our deepest fears, triggered sometimes by subconscious memories of a past-life relationship with them in which they caused us pain, or sometimes merely by their resemblance to an aggressor from earlier in our present life. In either case our instinctive reaction is to adopt the appropriate self-defence measures—with detrimental consequences both to the other person's well-being and to our relationship with them.

In the role of an outer planet we hold the key to the other person's happiness. Will we be successful in overcoming our deep-seated apprehensions or will we submit to our baser instincts? Will we be capable of expressing love towards them or will we seek to humiliate and destroy them to protect our own interests? It is down to us whether we bring joy or suffering into their lives: we are the instruments of their karma.

As the outer planet player our function is to teach the other individual something of the principle of love represented by the planet which we symbolize. The karmic destiny faced by the other individual is to meet with this principle, for good or for bad, in their relationship with us. The test faced by ourselves, as the embodiment of this principle, is to help the other individual come to terms with the lesson by the easy path or the rocky path.

Whatever our behaviour towards the other individual, they will, by karmic necessity, come to a greater understanding of the importance of a particular aspect of love, be this trust, support, forgiveness or letting go. But the ease with which they achieve this understanding and the degree to which they are able to discharge their karma is substantially dependent upon the awareness and enlightenment with which we play the outer planet role.

We owe it to ourselves to look very carefully at the way in which we choose to enact an outer planet in a personal relationship. Our choice will be liable not only to influence the other person's karma but, perhaps even more importantly, will have a bearing on the nature of our own.

In the positive outer planet role we assure our future good karma in the form of gifts and assets corresponding to the planet in question. In the negative role we condemn ourselves to a fate which obliges us to undergo precisely the same pain that we inflict on the other person in our present life.

By choosing the positive script, we consciously elect to derive the maximum potential from our casting and to initiate voluntarily the self-change possible within the relationship. Through our inter-action with the other player we are challenged to face and over-come our karmic fears—fears which inhibit us from tapping into the positive polarity of the planet, deprive us of love and deny us the opportunity to gain something of value from our relationship with the other person.

If, as outer planet players, we can abandon the defensive behaviour patterns which derive from our subconscious fears, we open ourselves up to the insights we can glean from the opposite player and to a spiritual learning process in which we are able to refine and develop our expression of the planetary energy.

It is only natural—and inevitable—that we should experience

some degree of fear when we enact an outer planet in a personal relationship. But how we handle that fear is critical in determining the quality of the relationship and the level of karmic healing and self-change that it is capable of producing.

Saturn

The planet Saturn can be considered as the police force in our solar system. Representing, as it does, the qualities of discipline and self-control, it exerts a civilizing influence on mankind, urging us to keep in check our more antisocial, anarchistic instincts.

This is the planetary energy which serves to maintain law and order in society by instilling us with a distaste for all behaviour likely to bring about disruptive change and threaten the established order. As such it plays a vital role in preserving the stable social framework necessary for any sustained concrete achievement and for the advancement of mankind in all spheres of life. Without Saturn we would lack the patience, concentration and organization required to materialize our goals.

But when Saturn's structuring influence is excessive, the urge to defer to the status quo becomes compulsive, overriding all other considerations and effectively crushing our originality of self-expression. In its negative polarity Saturn represents a reactionary governing force, opposed to all that is new, unconventional or imaginative and ultimately extinguishing every spark of human spirit. The scope of human endeavour becomes restricted to the pursuit of social standing, together with the necessary characteristics of ambition, rigid self-control and work mania.

Perhaps the most detrimental aspect of Saturn's negative polarity is its influence upon our spontaneity of expression. Preoccupation with success is inevitably flanked by fear of failure and the urge to align our actions with those most likely to reward us with the desired social status. Fired by this motivation we are likely to eliminate from our behaviour all that is socially unacceptable, thus repressing our most instinctive feelings whose free expression is essential to our health. Social acceptance is the criterion which governs our existence, even at the expense of our emotional and spiritual well-being. Social inadequacy is the insidious fear which casts a cloud over all areas of our life, as the natural joy of living is usurped by a permanent state of apprehension and self-consciousness.

In effect Saturn kills off the 'child' in us, sometimes long before the child is ready to die, urging us to eschew all frivolous or materially unproductive tendencies. It promotes the sensible 'grown-up' approach, vital of course in certain situations, but stultifying and soul-destroying without the necessary counter-balance of a little pure and simple fun.

Essentially the challenge of Saturn revolves around the notion of responsibility. In learning to handle this energy we must examine the nature and extent of our social obligations and the influence these exert on our potential for a truly fulfilling and happy life. Ultimately we are challenged to break free of the social conditioning which condemns us to the burden of cheerless duties, anxiety and depression.

In its purest form Saturn instils us with a sense of responsibility only to ourselves and a healthy disregard for the expectations of other people where these run counter to our personal convictions. It provides us with a level of self-containment which renders us immune to criticism or disapproval, thus assuring our serenity of mind. It engenders the independence and self-reliance necessary for the kind of concrete accomplishment associated with this planet at its best. At the heart of our practical abilities lies the keen sense of structure and organization characteristic of Saturn, but now these are enhanced by a degree of creative flexibility never possible when we are weighed down by social hang-ups.

In personal relationships also, cross-aspects involving Saturn are concerned with the development of a balanced sense of responsi-bility on the part of both individuals. The ease or difficulty with which this is achieved will depend on the attitudes of each person towards status and convention and their ability to break free from their social conditioning—reflected by the strength of Saturn by house, sign and aspect in their natal charts.

However, it is the outlook of the person who plays the Saturn role which has the greatest influence upon the ambiance of the relationship. To the extent that the Saturn individual is positively attuned to the vibrations of the planet, is uninfluenced by the demands of the status quo and has developed a true sense of self-reliance, he will be in a position to help the other person to achieve greater independence without the need to seek social approval.

In this mode the Saturn person plays the role of the firm but loving teacher from whom we can learn to be more disciplined, structured and organized—more productive in concrete terms. Learning can be relatively easy and enjoyable with this kind of instructor as there is no pressure to meet standards or fulfil expectations; nor are we subjected to criticism or ridicule when we find the lessons difficult. Whatever the form of the relationship, be it a teacher–pupil, lover–lover, parent–child or child–parent situation, the Saturn individual has the capacity to bring out the practical abilities of the other person by providing a supportive, stabilizing influence and by gently encouraging them towards ever greater levels of self-responsibility and achievement.

But it is unlikely that this loving, supportive help will be available if the Saturn person's own attitude towards responsibility is distorted. When the Saturn individual is himself unhealthily absorbed with the attainment of social standing and the maintenance of social standards, the likelihood is that, by projecting his social ambitions and hang-ups onto the other person, he will negatively influence their notions of obligation and duty within society.

Here the Saturn individual expresses the negative, unloving side of the planet, concerned as he is solely with his own needs rather than what would be really beneficial to the other person. This is the role of the narrow-minded, insensitive teacher who cruelly exposes the supposed weaknesses of pupils who fail to observe the norm.

We are unlikely to learn much from this kind of teacher who rules by fear and punishment, and in any type of personal relationship where the Saturn player fails to respect the right of the other person to express themselves with spontaneity and originality, there can be little prospect of any useful form of interchange.

Certainly we may be obliged to develop some level of self-sufficiency when we realize that no support—be it emotional, intellectual or practical—is available to us from the Saturn player and we are constantly thrown back on our own resources. But in many cases this is an ill-gained self-reliance marked by an embittered sense of neglect or ill treatment, negative expectations of future relationships in terms of genuine and loving support, and an ongoing resentment towards all authority-figures. Perhaps worst of all our self-confidence is likely to be deeply undermined so that success becomes a good deal more difficult for us to attain.

The icy criticism which is so often dispensed by the Saturn player and which is so detrimental to the self-assurance of his children, partners and associates, has its roots in his feelings of inadequacy—the inadequacy he experiences in the presence of another person who appears to possess some social asset which he believes he does not possess or which he is afraid to express. Driven by a primeval urge to hit out at that which causes him pain, he attempts to make the other person feel bad about the quality which they embody and which he is so painfully aware that he lacks. Generally he will seek to frustrate their expression of this quality—perhaps by ignoring or perhaps by actively criticizing them.

It seems that the other person's open expression of behaviour which would make him feel acutely self-conscious causes him as much embarrassment as if he were actually participating in this behaviour himself. And feelings of inadequacy and embarrassment do not engender a particularly supportive or encouraging response.

It is difficult to react positively when we are at the receiving end of the disapproval of a Saturn individual who is unwittingly projecting his own hang-ups onto us. Whatever the level of our abilities or our self-assurance, we may find ourselves succumbing to self-doubt in the face of his unrelenting lack of acknowledgement. The Saturn individual's sense of inadequacy can be catching, so that we too find that our creativity is undermined by inhibitions and anxiety.

Often we will do our best at first to fulfil the standards demanded of us by the Saturn player. But invariably our efforts are in vain and our final reaction may be to attempt to break free of this energy-sapping influence.

It is hardly surprising that tough Saturn cross-aspects can produce so much unhappiness in all types of personal relationships, but it need not necessarily be that way. Once we are aware of the roles we assume within a relationship, we can consciously choose to change our script and either person involved in the cross-aspect can be instrumental in making this transformation.

Ideally, of course, it should be the Saturn individual who takes the initiative since it is he who plays the leading role in the scenario and thus has the major influence. The first step for the Saturn player is to admit to himself that any difficulties in the relationship are most likely caused by his negative behaviour, behaviour provoked not by any failings on the part of the other person but by his own social hang-ups. As soon as the Saturn player is able to respect rather than condemn the opposite player's flexibility in the very area of self-expression about which he feels uptight, he opens himself to help from the other person in terms of learning by example.

Now the Saturn player may find that the roles are not as they initially appeared: the other person has as much if not more to teach him. True, the Saturn individual may well be able to help the other person become a more effective and acceptable member of society by instilling them with self-discipline and organization skills. But the opposite player can also change the Saturn individual's social attitudes by highlighting his excessive absorption with social acceptance and healing his crippling fear of ridicule and failure. The goal of this relationship is a balanced expression of social responsibility and the two players will rock the see-saw until that balance is finally reached.

A situation which often occurs in Saturn cross-aspects is that in which the Saturn player apparently involuntarily imposes a burden upon the other person, by his sickness or impecuniousness or some other disability, which obliges the other person to take on responsibilities over and above those which would normally be expected of them. In such cases the Saturn player has elected, prior to this incarnation, to serve as an instrument whereby the other player can redeem their karma through devoted care.

Even in this highly challenging scenario, the attitude of the Saturn player is critical in determining how comfortably the drama can unfold. Sometimes the Saturn player will be unable to resist exploiting his carer's sense of duty and commitment towards him with unreasonable demands and endless nagging. So that despite his pre-incarnational resolve to help them to discharge their karma with good grace, the Saturn player creates a set-up in which this becomes extremely difficult.

Whenever the Saturn person remains blind to his behaviour and motivation, it is important for the opposite player to use their own insight into the interaction to help defuse the situation. Once the opposite player understands the source of the Saturn individual's demands, they are less likely to retaliate and thus exacerbate the ill feeling. And once they understand that the Saturn player's criticism arises not from their own but from the Saturn player's shortcomings, they are more able to remain immune to his attacks and minimize the damage to their self-confidence.

Of course it may well be that despite their understanding of the situation, the opposite player simply will not wish to continue with a relationship which is bringing them no happiness or may decide that their karmic debt to the Saturn player has been discharged. In such cases, although the opposite player may terminate the relationship in order to protect themselves, they will do so without any trace of bitterness or hatred. They thus sever their karmic link to the Saturn individual whatever the latter's state of mind towards them. They may indeed meet with the Saturn player again in a future life, but they will no longer feel attachment to him—they will be free of his influence.

How often do we learn too late, when we play the Saturn role, that we have driven away the very person we love and need; that our inability to show our appreciation of them has robbed us of the role model which could have helped us to overcome our inhibitions. When we play Saturn, the permanence of the relationship lies essentially in our control. We may lose a loved one for ever unless we are prepared to give concrete expression to that love by placing the needs of the other person before our own fears, anxieties and self-consciousness.

Uranus

The planet Uranus stands for freedom. It helps to liberate us from excessive preoccupation with the duties which we feel obliged to carry out under the influence of Saturn and which can sometimes restrict us unduly. Uranus prevents us from becoming stuck in a rut: it provides the stimulus for us to seek out new experiences continually and to experiment with that which is different.

Unlike Saturn, Uranus has no time whatsoever for the status quo. It delights in breaking with convention and outraging conservative opinion. The energy of Uranus urges us to forgo behaviour patterns which result simply from our social conditioning in favour of true creativity. It impels us to express our individuality regardless of whether this is acceptable to others or not. And in freeing us from the strait-jacket of conformism, it allows us to express ourselves inventively and with originality in all areas of life.

Indeed, Uranus symbolizes the source from which all 'new' ideas arise.

Ultimately, under the influence of Uranus we learn to accept not only our own individuality but that of every human being. We become tolerant of all modes of thought and behaviour, even where these are totally opposed to our own. We acquire a degree of adaptability which allows us to mix freely with people of every colour, class, age and creed and thus to expand constantly our understanding of life.

The ability to move around at will, untethered by attachments to other individuals or to material possessions, is essential if we are to take advantage of all opportunities to widen our horizons. But in some cases the level of our detachment and desire for freedom becomes excessive, destroying our ability to respond sensitively and with commitment to others.

In its negative polarity Uranus leads us to a state of constant flux in which continuity and stability—of behaviour, thought or feeling—become impossible. A constant urge for excitement and a fear of restriction override all other considerations and prevent us from approaching any situation with a view to long-term involvement. Projects thus become extremely difficult to complete.

The exaggerated resentment of authority and desire for social equality associated with Uranus in its negative polarity ultimately jeopardizes our ability to operate effectively in society, making it hard for us to follow orders and sometimes leading to a compulsive and inappropriate rebelliousness.

Often there is an irrepressible urge to flaunt convention by any means, however distasteful, as an immature expression of our individuality. And when our ideas and beliefs are insufficiently developed, perverse argumentativeness may be the only manifestation of our unwillingness to conform to the status quo.

The challenge represented by the planet Uranus is to be true to ourselves as individuals whilst simultaneously respecting the right of others to their own form of self-expression. We are encouraged to do our own thing, but only in so far as the pursuit of freedom is not detrimental to others. Under the influence of Uranus we learn to break down the barriers of prejudice which separate us from other people and inhibit our understanding of the universe. And it is primarily through relationships of as manifold and diverse a nature as possible that this process of growth takes place.

The function of Uranus cross-aspects in chart comparisons is to expand our consciousness by introducing some new, untried experience into our life. Uranus relationships are based on the theme of mutual discovery, whereby each person can bring out the originality and uniqueness in the other. For this reason, first meetings are always marked by a sense of tremendous excitement in subconscious anticipation of the revelations about to unfold. Uranus cross-aspects are also concerned with mutual liberation and independence, whereby each person encourages the other to function as a separate autonomous entity, free of any restraints which social convention might impose.

When we play the role of Uranus in a chart comparison, the greatest gift we can give to the other person is to allow them the freedom to develop as an individual whilst providing them with ongoing loving support. The greatest gift we can receive from them is the insight of their personal outlook on life—provided we have the humility to accept it. The degree to which we will achieve this is dependent upon our own level of attunement to Uranus and on the extent to which we respect other human beings as equals.

When we accept the right of all men and women to do their own thing, however bizarre, we will delight in and encourage the other person's idiosyncracies as an expression of their uniqueness. It comes naturally to us to support them in making their mark on the world. But when we view life purely from our own standpoint and are fearful of ideas and behaviour which differ from our own, we are likely to ridicule any self-expression on their part which we find unacceptable or incomprehensible. This is an approach which is unhelpful not only to them but also to ourselves, since we deny ourselves the opportunity to learn something new and of value.

Equally, when we acknowledge the right of all mankind to enjoy the same measure of liberty, we will find it relatively easy to allow the other person their freedom rather than expecting them to acquiesce in our wishes. But if we place our own independence before that of others, we are likely to remain blind to the other person's need for freedom, with the result that they feel there is one rule for us and another for them.

When we play the role of 'bad-guy' Uranus in a relationship, some of our most unpleasant traits derive from over-detachment. Because we are unable to understand where the other person is coming from, we are insensitive to their emotional, physical and intellectual needs, and find it difficult to respond intimately to them at any of these levels. We may well be free of the possessiveness and desire for control which arise from over-attachment, but when we are entirely lacking in empathy, the relationship is likely to be played at a very superficial level.

That is not to say that we do not enjoy the other person's company, but simply that we have no deep or permanent need of it. The exhilaration of free discovery is more important to us than the comfort of long-term security and we may find it impossible to resist the desire to move on, even if this means hurting other people's feelings. In some cases we will terminate a relationship when it loses its attraction; in others we may continue the relationship on an intermittent basis with the aim of recapturing some of the original sparkle.

It is this intermittent physical—or perhaps just emotional and mental—absenteeism which is often most difficult to live with in a relationship with someone who plays the role of Uranus. Harder still, the absenteeism is likely to be totally unpredictable, since any form of order or regularity is repellent to Uranus. In the negative Uranus mode we are likely to be unpredictable not only in our behaviour but also in our thoughts and feelings, which can seem confusing and hurtful to those who love us and depend upon us for their security. In some cases the Uranus player's high-speed turnover of response can seem utterly irrational to the other individual and can be experienced as destabilizing and deeply shocking.

When our Uranus forms a challenging aspect with a personal planet or angle in another person's chart, we are often unable to carry through any sustained line of thought, which makes it hard for us to conduct a reasonable conversation. Our communication skills are also likely to be hampered by our scornful disagreement with any sentiment we do not currently share.

The exaggerated independence we so often display when we play the role of Uranus is motivated by the fear that, unless we resist very hard, the relationship may somehow deprive us of our much-prized freedom. At a subconscious level we feel threatened by the ideas, behaviour or emotions of the other person which as yet we do not understand but which we experience as sufficiently seductive to jeopardize our freewheeling non-commitment.

At one level we are enticed and excited by what the other person represents, but at another level we are fearful of becoming ensnared by them and are careful to maintain our emotional, mental or physical distance. It is this juxtaposition of fascination and fear which lies behind the Uranus player's inconsistent response and which manifests as alternating attraction and detachment.

When we find ourselves subjected to this kind of unpredictable behaviour by the Uranus player, it can be hard for us to comprehend his inexplicable reversals of attitude and we are often both bewildered and resentful. How are we to come to terms with someone who on one occasion seems spellbound by our company but on another appears totally indifferent; who initially is fascinated by our ideas and sentiments but later dismisses them with contempt and ridicule; who at one time seems unable to bear a moment out of our presence but at other times is nowhere to be found, especially when we need him most?

When we are emotionally attached to the Uranus individual our instinctive response is to try to hold him close to us to maintain the elation we experience in his company and to prevent him from abandoning us, which we fear is a strong possibility. But it is a response which is doomed to failure on two counts. Firstly, it is never possible to chain down the wilful, freedom-seeking Uranus player and any attempt will be swiftly countered by entrenched and bloody-minded rebellion. Secondly, since the fun and exhilaration associated with a Uranus cross-aspect are spasmodic by their very nature, their manifestation is dependent upon an intermittent association; monotony and stability are likely to extinguish every spark of excitement and to rapidly kill the relationship stone dead.

When another person's Uranus forms a hard aspect with a personal planet or angle in our chart, we are challenged to express true love for him by allowing him his freedom and reducing our dependence upon him. At first we may fear that in so doing we risk losing him, but invariably this is not so. Provided he is allowed to do so of his own volition, the Uranus player will return to us repeatedly and perhaps for ever more in order to recapture periodically that incomparable thrill.

Ultimately, of course, we have no choice other than to sever our attachment and to build a life of our own, since the Uranus player cannot be possessed and to a greater or lesser extent will leave us to our own devices. But it is far better for us, and for him, if we can let go of our own free will and in a spirit of loving acceptance.

It is a great deal easier to be lovingly acceptant of the Uranian's comings and goings if he in turn is lovingly acceptant of our own needs and weaknesses. It is always necessary for the Uranus player to bear in mind that he holds the trump card in determining our happiness and security. Notwithstanding his affection for us, usually the Uranus player is emotionally uninvolved and unlikely to undergo profound suffering whatever the outcome of the relationship; we, however, may well be deeply reliant upon him and more sensitive to his mistreatment than he is able to appreciate.

Despite the characteristic tendency of the Uranus player to spurn responsibility, unless he is willing to approach the relationship with some sense of obligation and commitment, the prospect of happiness is bleak. The challenge of the Uranus player is to accept that freedom must co-exist alongside of responsibility, if it is not to be destructive of human happiness and love. Somewhere deep in his psyche resides a karmic fear of losing his liberty. This is the fear that can lead him to resist contemptuously any new idea which might necessitate serious reconsideration. This too is the fear that causes him to shy away wildly from any form of ongoing involvement and which he must learn to overcome, if he is not to spend incarnation after incarnation haunted by a dread of restraint.

The pursuit of personal freedom can prove lonely and empty unless it is complemented by the warmth and companionship of loving human contact. Conversely the closest of relationships can become stifling and unfulfilling unless counterbalanced by an independent existence in one's own right. When two individuals are drawn together by karma in a Uranus cross-aspect, their task is to work towards achieving this delicate balance.

Neptune

All that is beautiful and uplifting in life, all that is noble, altruistic and selfless in human nature derives from the planet Neptune. Neptune is the refining force which lifts us above purely material or egotistical concerns; it symbolizes our spiritual identity as opposed to our baser, animalistic instincts.

Under the influence of this planet's vibrations mundane affairs lose their attraction and we begin to reach out for more soul-satisfying experiences which touch the very core of our being. When Neptune is strongly placed in our birth chart we crave a level of emotional fulfilment which is difficult to attain in the three-dimensional world. Essentially we are seeking a sense of at-oneness with the entire universe rather than with any isolated element thereof, for it is only when we experience ourselves as part of a greater whole that we satisfy our spiritual hunger.

The Neptunian yearning for ecstasy is difficult to assuage other than by mystical practices such as meditation and yoga; however, music, art and drama also allow us to raise our consciousness and lose ourselves in something larger than our own reality.

Neptune instils us with an idealism which is content only with the very finest in life and in ourselves and which renders us susceptible to frequent disappointments and guilt. At best we can learn to work with our ideals through a process of creative visualization to help bring them into being at the material level. By purposively focusing only on the purest qualities in ourselves, in others, and in the world about us, we reinforce these qualities in our awareness and thus experience a greater sense of joy and inner peace.

Often, however, we find it difficult to cast off the painful disillusionment which can overshadow our perception of life when nothing and nobody, including ourselves, lives up to our expectations. Sooner or later we come to believe that our dreams cannot materialize in real life and turn instead to a fantasy world in which we create our own reality. In some cases we use alcohol and drugs to gain access to this world, but in other cases the power of our imagination is sufficient to transport us.

Depending upon the extent of our despair, we can sometimes lose touch completely with normality, finding it difficult to distinguish between fact and fiction. As ever, the influence of Neptune allows us to step readily out of the three-dimensional world, but for this planet to function safely in our consciousness we need to keep our feet planted firmly on the ground.

Neptune challenges us to break down the barriers which separate us from others at the emotional level, so that we are able to feel for and empathize with them. But to avoid becoming swamped by extraneous emotions and losing our sense of personal identity, it is essential that we maintain some boundary line between ourselves and the outside world. It is important that we should be able to distinguish clearly those feelings which are inherently ours and those which are not. The planet Neptune urges us to step out of ourselves to experience an emotional at-oneness with others, but only provided we are securely anchored in our own individuality.

Only when we are able to retain a strong sense of ourselves as a separate being are we able to express our compassion for human pain and suffering in an effective manner. When our sense of 'self' is insufficiently developed, we risk over-identifying with others and reacting over-sensitively to their problems.

When our Neptune forms a cross-aspect with a personal planet or angle in another person's chart, the sensitivity associated with Neptune can produce a personal relationship which we believe to be based on a deep emotional rapport and an almost telepathic link. We often feel that the other person seems part of ourselves, which leads to an unusual sense of closeness but can also cause us serious problems in terms of projection. Our heightened emotional awareness of the other person can create a deep level of intimacy, but can also lead us to modify our behaviour towards them in a manner which is mutually detrimental.

When we consider ourselves to be finely attuned to another person's emotional and mental reactions, honesty is likely to be our greatest difficulty. Invariably we are tempted to bend the truth a little in order to spare them the pain of discovering the real facts—pain which we suppose they might suffer but which actually may be no more than a figment of our imagination.

When, in a Neptune cross-aspect, we are unclear about the dividing line between our own reality and the reality of the other person, we are prone to project onto them feelings and reactions which are essentially our own. So that in attempting to protect them from what we believe would be an unhappy experience, we are merely responding to our own assessment of the situation. In effect we may have no comprehension whatsoever of what their true reactions might be.

Always, with Neptune, there is the urge to experience at-oneness with others and often the belief that we do so, but real ability to achieve this at-oneness is rare and we fool ourselves if we think otherwise.

The lies and falsehoods which we often concoct when we play Neptune in order to 'spare the feelings' of the other person can produce, at the final count, a devastating sense of betrayal on their part. The comment 'I didn't tell you because I didn't want to hurt you' is unlikely to prove much comfort to an individual who has suffered far more as a result of the Neptune player's deceit than if they had known the plain truth from the start.

The issue of projection is fundamental to all relationships involving a Neptune cross-aspect. When we play Neptune we are likely to project upon the other person not only our unconscious thoughts and feelings, but all our unrealized aspirations, ambitions and goals in life. We may invest in the other person all those aspects of ourselves which we have as yet been unable to fulfil, whether or not they embody such traits. We fall into the trap of seeing them as an unacknowledged and as yet unexpressed extension of ourselves, rather than the separate and unique human being which they really are.

When we base a relationship on our observation of someone not as they are but only as we would like them to be, we embark on a rocky course. Sooner or later, when the veil falls from our eyes, we must face the true nature of the other person rather than our idealized perception of them and we are likely to complain bitterly of disillusionment.

In a Neptune cross-aspect both players may eventually come to believe that the other person has changed in some way from how they appeared originally and therefore has let them down. The Neptune player invariably fails to realize that when he sees the other person in a different light, it is as a result of a shift in his own awareness rather than a change of character or behaviour on the part of the opposite player. The opposite player has more justification in complaining of a change of attitude in the Neptune player when he finally awakes from his fantasy. When we receive the brunt of someone's disappointment in us, and for no good reason other than their own neurosis, it is difficult not to feel let down by their altered response, and in some cases the withdrawal of their 'love'.

Personal relationships involving Neptune are frequently subject to tremendous surges of elation and despair, of romanticism and cold realism and of idealization and disillusionment. To spare ourselves such emotional extremes we need to ensure that however much we love or are in love with another person, we remain aware of their shortcomings. That we view them not as gods but as fragile mortals capable, just like ourselves, of making mistakes, committing sins and breaking hearts.

When we play Neptune in a cross-aspect, our toughest task is to resist the tendency to place the other person on a pedestal, expecting them to live out for us some hero or heroine role which they cannot possibly fulfil. Certainly we are challenged to look for the best in them and to view them as far as possible in a good light, for the role of Neptune is always to focus on the positive and thus bring it closer to fulfilment. But we are also challenged to accept them as whole people by acknowledging their shadow and their darkness as well as their beauty and their light.

The Neptune player in a cross-aspect is also liable to expect far too much from himself in the relationship, setting himself impossible behaviour standards as spouse, parent or child, and criticizing himself for failing to meet those standards. For this reason the Neptune player often carries an oppressive sense of guilt which casts a shadow over the potential joy of the relationship and may eventually lead him to end the relationship in order to rescue his battered self-worth.

In other cases Neptune will seek to assuage his guilt by martyring himself in the service of the loved one, often placing himself at the mercy of an unscrupulous partner, parent or child who will bleed him dry. When Neptune allows himself to be used in this way, he further damages his self-esteem and the burden he creates for himself can lead to resentment towards the other person and the possible breakdown of the relationship.

The trouble with Neptune is that when he feels aggrieved, he cannot openly express his pain to the other person since he is afraid to rock the boat. In a futile attempt to live up to a saint-like image he tries to gloss over the bad and the ugly, but invariably ends up by expressing his resentments out of earshot of the other person and succumbing to deviousness, treachery and back-stabbing.

Neptune may also resort to various types of escapism as a passive form of protest. Occasionally he will just disappear overnight without excuse or explanation, leaving behind a distraught and bewildered lover or relative who genuinely had no idea that anything was wrong. Emotional withdrawal is another Neptunian ploy, as is alcohol and drug abuse, suicide or even degenerative illness, brought on perhaps by feelings of powerlessness.

The Neptunian philosophy of 'turning the other cheek'—of

putting up with unhappiness without complaint—simply doesn't work in real life. A balanced, healthy relationship demands clear and honest feedback on both sides, something that can never happen when Neptune makes a victim of himself. Before he can ever respect and love another person, Neptune must acquire some respect and love for himself.

Essential to the principle of Neptune is the ability to forgive both others and ourselves, a quality likely to be frequently called upon in a cross-aspect based on this planet. Both participants will be required to express forgiveness when their hopes of the other person, themselves, or the relationship are disappointed and when the falsehood inherent in the contact is unmasked.

Every Neptune cross-aspect involves an element of deception, a tendency to see ourselves, the other person or the relationship in a false light rather than as they actually are. When we play Neptune, ours is the key role in determining the degree of that deception and the likely disillusionment. To minimize the sense of mutual let-down it is essential that we aim for scrupulous truth-fulness in the relationship, both with ourselves and with the other person, although Neptune's reluctance to face the bare facts can make this a constant struggle.

Our difficulty, when we play Neptune, is to live out the rela-tionship above the level of the banal without deviating into the realms of the unreal. Nearly always there is a strong desire to elevate the union onto some higher, mystical plane which will provide both ourselves and the other person with euphoric fulfilment. Sometimes we will seek to achieve this fulfilment through drink, drugs or perverted sex, activities which give us a temporary buzz but are ultimately degrading. At other times we may eschew all physical contact with the other person in the assumption that sexual or emotional self-denial is an essential component of spirituality. Each of these approaches can be painful to both players and ultimately damaging to the relationship.

The fundamental challenge for the Neptune player is to uplift the relationship—and his partner—without detriment to either person and so as to bring only beauty and joy into their lives. In many cases he is able to help the other person towards higher levels of consciousness by introducing them to the arts, music, or religious concepts, or by encouraging them to be more com-passionate. But often Neptune can bring out the best in the opposite player simply by positive visualization—by affirming their strengths whilst accepting their weaknesses and thus loving them unconditionally.

Unconditional love forms the basis of all Neptune cross-aspects, whether between romantic partners or parents and children. For the Neptune individual the challenge is to love without any preconceptions as to how he would like things to be and without suffering any sense of let-down. For the opposite player also, the challenge is that of loving regardless, of pardoning the delusions, deceptions and betrayals of Neptune, and where necessary giving him another chance.

If the players in a Neptune drama are to survive without breaking each other's hearts, they must each learn to overcome disillusion-ment and to forgive. When love is unconditional there can be no disillusionment since we have no prior expectations. And when we love someone in spite of everything, forgiving is easy because basically there is nothing to forgive.

Pluto

The most powerful force for good or evil on earth—this is the planet Pluto. Pluto is associated with extremes—extremes of feeling, extremes of attitude and extremes of behaviour.

Under the influence of Pluto we can succumb to the depths of depression, frustration and bitterness, we can experience a com-pulsive desire for power born of insecurity and fear of loss, and we can commit the most cruel and ruthless deeds in order to further our own ends, destroying everything that stands in our way.

Yet Pluto is also associated with the highest levels of emotional and spiritual well-being, with a joyful approach to life in the expectation that all our needs will be met, and with the willingness to use all our resources to bring healing and abundance to the planet as a whole.

Through a process of metamorphosis triggered by Pluto, we can find ourselves magically transformed from 'sinners' to 'saints', our experience of life can change from something approaching hell to something closer to heaven, and the planet earth can become a place for wholeness and healing rather than destruction, war and suffering.

The transmutation we can undergo when we open ourselves to

Pluto is both simple and immensely demanding. The sole requirement is that we let go of our insecurity, our anger and our obsessive desire to maintain control; yet when such behaviour is inbuilt into our psyche, having been inculcated over many incarnations, it can prove stubbornly resistant to dislodgement.

The Pluto-linked wholeness and well-being that we can bring about in ourselves and in others is nevertheless dependent upon our ability to discharge the negative emotions and attitudes which sap so much of our vital energy. Only when we release this negativity do we gain full access to the restorative power of our life-force, which has within itself the potential to cure all ills and to turn our darkness into brilliant light.

In order to accomplish this process of letting go, it is important that we are able to perceive our fears and their sources; that we are able to acknowledge the controlling, manipulative tendencies which derive from these fears; and that we can admit to the defensiveness and lack of trust that hold us back from opening up fully to other human beings and to life's glorious potential for growth. All too often we remain stubbornly blind to our shadow, but unless we have the courage to confront ourselves with honesty, there can never be any question of positive self-change or self-healing.

Clarity of insight is perhaps our most valuable transformational tool. Accurate perception of those psychological patterns, in ourselves and in others, which have become outworn and are in need of renewal is an essential prerequisite for any kind of healing process. For this reason Pluto is associated with all studies and therapies which provide us firstly with self-knowledge and secondly with the ability to help others attain greater personal awareness.

The power to diagnose is an asset which equips us for many forms of investigative and research work, particularly in science and medicine, but which can also be exploited at a more profound level to trigger positive change in our environment whenever and wherever there is deadlock.

Crucial to Pluto is the ability to eliminate. Failure to do so condemns us to a physical, mental and emotional stagnation, which not only prevents us from moving on at the appropriate time but is also likely to lead to an insidious poisoning of our bodies and minds.

The ability to let go psychologically is also of vital importance if we are to avoid over-possessiveness, over-attachment and the associated destructive behaviour patterns which can choke the life out of even the strongest relationship. All too often we confuse love with control and domination and believe that our compulsion to hang on to another human being come what may is a manifestation of our affection for them. However, the role of Pluto in personal relationships is to teach us that this is not so, and that it is only when we break free of our emotional dependency on another person that we are able to express our genuine love for them and to bring real joy and wholeness into both their life and our own.

When we play Pluto in a cross-aspect involving that planet, we are destined to make a powerful impact on the other person and to bring about some far-reaching change in their life. Our ultimate challenge is to provide them with helpful insights into long-standing attitudes which derive from subconscious insecurities and are now detrimental to their well-being.

The good Pluto player serves as a mirror which gently reveals the opposite player's vulnerabilities and supplies them with the strength to instigate the appropriate self-change. The good Pluto player gives truthful feedback but only when this is likely to be helpful and never so as to cause pointless suffering. And the good Pluto player never attempts to force change onto another person against their wishes or to mould them according to personal desires. The positive function of Pluto is to open the door for the other individual, not to push them through it against their will.

But we will find it difficult to play the positive Pluto role in a relationship unless we have at least partially come to terms with the challenges of this planet at a personal level. If we are unable to recognize our own vulnerabilities, how can we help another person towards any kind of self-knowledge? If we ourselves are fixed and inflexible, how can we encourage someone else to cast off the old and welcome the new? If our own lives are stunted and overshadowed by dependencies and compulsions, what use can we be to another human being in terms of helping them to let go?

The truth is that until we have confronted our own fears and moved some way towards overcoming our own attachments, we have nothing whatsoever to offer. The unenlightened Pluto player invariably projects all of his subconscious insecurities onto the other person, with devastating consequences for both parties.

When we play the negative Pluto role, we unwittingly perceive the other person as a symbol of whatever traits we are most reluctant to face in ourselves. We fear them for their open expression of those traits and their power to confront us with our weaknesses. And we fear them because they may trigger a transformation of our personality which will inevitably cause us pain. In a few cases there is some justification to our fears inasmuch as the other person represents a genuine threat to our security. But mostly our fears are without foundation and result purely from our unconscious projections.

The instinctive Plutonic urge to overpower that which menaces us impels us to defend ourselves from danger by dominating the individual who embodies that danger. Ensuring control over the opposite player now becomes paramount and we will attempt to maintain our control by any means at our disposal, including manipulation, bullying and blackmail. In romantic relationships we may convince ourselves that we 'love' the other person, that we need them because we care about them and have a genuine affection for them. But in reality we simply fear them, we care nothing for them as individuals and we desire to keep them close to us only to protect our own vulnerability.

We feel subconsciously threatened by any change which might prise the opposite player from our grip and will ruthlessly resist such change, even where this is clearly to their disadvantage. In effect we are obsessed and our obsession renders us blind to the real needs of the other player and of our relationship with them.

Whatever power we possess will be used to safeguard our own needs, even at the risk of wounding or inflicting harm on the object of our attachment. Whatever insights we possess will be exploited to manipulate the 'loved one' into complying with our wishes. Whatever home truths we dispense will be designed to belittle their ideas or achievements, to bolster our threatened ego and to perpetuate our own sense of control. All in the name of love the negative Pluto player can do a very good job of convincing the other person that in reality he hates them.

When we are the victim of a Pluto player's obsession it is difficult for us to believe his claims that the possessiveness and manipulation to which we are so often subjected stem from his 'affection' for us. Ultimately the effect of such controlling behaviour is to cause us to feel that we are imprisoned, that we are suffocating, and that we must escape as far away as possible. Sometimes we will cut ourselves off physically, sometimes emotionally, but the end result is often that we break away irrevocably from the Pluto player's hold upon us. The Pluto player is now defeated by his own tactics, driving away, through his domination and his fixity, the very person he has greatest need of and has sought so hard to hold on to.

The act of letting go forms the main scenario in the drama enacted by the two individuals in a Pluto cross-aspect and each must come to terms with this process in their own way. As 'victims' we will find it more or less difficult to make the break, depending upon the condition of our own chart. If our Uranus is strong, we will desire to free ourselves sooner than if we are more attuned to dutiful Saturn or if we too have a powerful Pluto and find it hard to let go. But in every case there is some level of attachment, developed during many incarnations in the company of the Pluto player, and we must not underestimate our complicity in our present situation. Our dependence upon the Pluto player may be inbuilt into our psyche, and breaking the karmic pattern can require a great deal of will-power on our part.

But it is often the Pluto player who faces the hardest task in letting go when he is rejected by an exasperated partner, friend or relative. Often, when we play Pluto, we may have no choice other than to relinquish another individual as a result of their physical departure from our lives, but we may still find it difficult to abandon our emotional and psychological attachment to them. Indeed this attachment can continue unchecked for many years following the rupture, generating a sense of bitterness and desire for revenge which can contaminate every aspect of our existence. Physical release of another individual is not the important issue—it is only when we release them emotionally and psychologically that we give them their freedom, demonstrate our real love for them and simultaneously discover a previously unexploited aspect of our own creativity.

There is no reason at all why Pluto cross-aspects should involve physical separation; this only becomes necessary when the intensity of the Pluto player's hold is too threatening to both players' well-being. Ideally the Pluto player can learn to 'let go' of the other individual within the framework of a continuing relationship which is based on genuine, non-invasive love and which is the source of a powerful, mutually regenerating energy.

By abandoning the need for control over the other person, the Pluto player also allows himself access to greater self-awareness. When the opposite player no longer poses a threat, the Pluto player can actually begin to listen to what they have to say, to look at what they represent, and to acknowledge that he may have something to learn from them.

In a healthy Pluto cross-aspect the relationship can be a vehicle for self-change on the part of both participants. It is the role of the Pluto player both to give and to receive personal insights, to stimulate transformation in the other player and to undergo transformation himself.

A Pluto cross-aspect represents a two-way lesson in the conquest of fear, the development of trust, and the ability to relinquish the need for control. It is primarily through Pluto relationships that we face the immense challenge of learning to let go. And it is through Pluto that we make the greatest progress in understanding the true essence of love.

The love we learn to express in Pluto relationships is not possessive but liberating; it cannot remain static but must forever change its form. And through Pluto we come to realize that despite its uncertainty, love need never involve suffering—it is joyful, not sorrowful, it is creative, not destructive, and it is regenerative not depletive. It is through the love ruled by Pluto that we bring greater light and healing into our lives and gain access to the energy to spread light and healing throughout the planet as a whole.

Common to all of the outer planets is a pattern of fear and defensive behaviour, triggered by the personality of the inner planet player. Fundamental to this fear is the belief that the inner planet player is liable to affect them so profoundly that a tremendous change may occur in their lives.

Each outer planet is worried about losing what currently constitutes his reality—Saturn his social conditioning, Uranus his independence, Neptune his ideals and Pluto his security—and the psychological trauma this would involve. Each outer planet will also adopt the appropriate defence tactics to stem the threat from the inner planet player and 'keep them in their place', Saturn by criticism, Uranus by detachment and ridicule, Neptune by delusion and Pluto by ruthless manipulation.

Saturn, whose fear is that the inner planet player may draw attention to his social inadequacies, will attempt to protect himself by focusing instead on the inner planet player's own inadequacies.

Uranus, afraid that the other person will oblige him to change his thinking, will become overly distanced from the other person and cast scorn on their ideas as an instinctive defence mechanism.

For Neptune, the subconscious fear is that the inner planet player will oblige him to look at his pain and disappointment in the cold light of day, a fear which he tries to prevent from materializing by evading reality in his dealings with the other person.

And Pluto's reaction to the paralysing fear that the inner planet player may force him to confront his inability to let go is to try to adopt a position of complete control which rules out any possibility of loss.

The common challenge of the outer planets is to work through this process of fear to a position of clarity and enlightenment in which they are willing to accept and benefit from the self-change they can experience at the hands of the inner planet player. Before this can happen, each outer planet player must be willing to open himself fully to the inner planet player and to discontinue his defensive behaviour.

Thus Saturn must be prepared to stop criticizing the other person if he is to learn to overcome his social hang-ups with their help. Uranus must be willing to stop ridiculing and move closer to the other person if he is to receive mental stimulation from them, which will expand his horizons. Not until Neptune stops deluding himself and others will he be capable of coping with his disillusionment and of expressing unconditional love for the other individual. And not until Pluto steps down from the position of control will he be receptive to the powerful insights the other person can trigger in him and to the self-healing which can ensue.

Furthermore, it is only when the outer planets abandon their defence tactics that they can claim their true role of spiritual teachers and help the inner planet players to meet their karma in a positive way. When this happens, a two-way growth process begins to unfold, in which outer and inner planet player are able to learn from one another in a loving interchange.

The Saturn player will then find that not only can he become more socially adept with the help of the inner planet person, but he in turn can help them to become more effective in society. The Uranus player will not only be stimulated by the ideas of the inner planet person, but will himself be able to activate the inner planet person's mind. The Neptune player and the inner planet player can help one another to be more selfless in their expression of love. And the Pluto player and his partner can share mutual insights which promote their spiritual growth.

This two-way process of exchange can never happen when the outer planet player is operating from a position of fear or aggression, for however much he may believe he has to teach the inner planet player, none of us will listen to the kind of teacher who criticizes, ridicules, bullies or ignores us. When we play the role of an outer planet, it is our challenge to ensure that we play the type of teacher who teaches wisely and kindly and who recognizes, above all, that he has much to learn from his pupil.

THE ROLES OF THE INNER PLANETS IN INTERPERSONAL RELATIONSHIPS

Every chart comparison will be characterized by two or three major cross-aspects, in which we are likely to play the role of at least one outer planet and at least one inner planet. In one area of the relationship we may find that it is we ourselves who are dominant and are thus assigned the role of the outer planet, whereas in another area it may be our parent, partner, friend or even our child who assumes the controlling role.

Whereas the roles of the outer planets are active and are largely responsible for writing the script of the relationship, the inner planets and the chart angles are more passive factors which, at least initially, are receptive to and influenced by the energies of the outer planets.

The prime function of the outer planets is to give and that of the inner planets to receive. The outer planet player is the teacher, whereas the inner planet player is the pupil. The individual symbolizing the outer planet dispenses the karma; the individual symbolizing the inner planet submits to the karma. It is through the medium of the outer planet player that the inner planet player meets with his past-life behaviour patterns and receives the opportunity to release and transform those patterns.

When several cross-aspects occur between inner and outer planets in a chart comparison, the two individuals nearly always have a long karmic history behind them. They have lived a number of past lives in close contact with one another, sometimes in a sexual partnership, sometimes in a nurturing or sibling relationship. But in each case they have adopted the same planetary roles in relation to one another, acting out the same karmic drama and invariably failing to break their bondage to one another.

Relationships which extend so far back into time forge powerful mutual attachments, attachments which are experienced in particular by the inner planet player, who becomes accustomed to the outer planet player's dominance in the relationship and dependent upon his guidance and control, however difficult the past-life interaction may have been.

When the two people meet again for the first time in a new incarnation, this dependence is experienced by the inner planet player as a strong and irresistible attraction, often together with an inexplicable emotional hunger. Such feelings may be accompanied by apprehension or even definite dislike, despite which the inner planet player usually finds it extremely hard just to walk away. He may or may not be aware of the powerful hold that the outer planet player exerts over him—a hold which has its roots in past-life reliance and in this life will make it extremely difficult for him to terminate the relationship voluntarily.

Both participants in a karmic relationship are likely to experience their fair share of fear. For the inner planet player this fear is likely to centre around his long-standing association with the outer planet player and his need to maintain their presence—however painful—in his life. It is this unwillingness to face the future without the old familiar relationship pattern, even where it is clearly detrimental, which makes it so hard for the inner planet player to break free.

When we play the inner planet role, our destiny is to meet our karma at the hands of the outer planet player. Inevitably this is likely to involve some suffering for us as we are confronted, through the other person's behaviour, with the psychological and emotional pain we have previously inflicted on others. But this need not mean that we are destined to suffer for ever, and the sooner we are able to learn the karmic lesson, the sooner we can release ourselves from our bondage to the outer planet player and from the incessant repetition of an unproductive or destructive relationship pattern.

If we find ourselves in a compulsive relationship with an outer planet individual who persistently treats us badly, who remains blind to their negative behaviour towards us and who is unwilling to change, there is still a lot that we can do to deal effectively with the situation and to minimize our karmic pain.

First and foremost it is well to remember that whatever ill

treatment we undergo at the hands of an outer planet individual, this only reflects our own attunement to the planetary energy and our own past-life attitudes to others. However difficult it may be for us to admit it, the truth is that we only ever meet with ourselves in the outer planet player, or at least with our own unacknowledged traits symbolized by the outer planet. This awareness allows us to depersonalize the problem, to centre our disapproval upon the deed rather than the doer, and to recognize that the outer planet player is no more than an instrument whereby we can face, discharge and transform our own karma.

Also of value is the ability to understand the motivation of the outer planet player—the insecurities which lie at the root of his self-defensive or aggressive behaviour and which originate from his own earlier suffering. Perhaps we remind him of a figure from his childhood who caused him loss or anguish or threatened his well-being in some way. Or perhaps we ourselves were responsible for inflicting pain upon him in some past-life scenario and in some different relationship guise.

What we can be sure of, however, is that the outer planet player's mistreatment of us is always governed by fear, a fear of being crushed, hurt, or having his weaknesses exposed, a fear which may be triggered by our personality, by our vibrations or simply by the archetypal figure which we represent.

It is only natural that we should experience anger and indignation when, as an inner planet player, we are subjected to negative karmic treatment at the hands of the other person. Indeed it would be detrimental to our psychological and physical health if we were to suppress that anger or fail to give it a proper outlet. But when this is done, we can put our resentment aside and view our situation with a new enlightenment; we can start to release our negative karma, and take the first step along the path of self-healing.

We will realize the utter futility of a tit-for-tat approach. Revenge, whatever form it takes, only condemns us to further karmic retribution of the same ilk or introduces a new karmic debt. Attempting to settle the score can provide us with temporary satisfaction, but this may be outweighed by the future problems which we are inevitably setting up for ourselves.

When we play an inner planet, we can promote the self-healing process by self-awareness and self-change. Once we are able to acknowledge the outer planet player's behaviour in ourselves, once we begin to refine the associated planetary energy, we find that we are no longer so affected by his misuse of that energy even when it continues to be directed towards us. We may still be aware of and condemn his negativity, but now it will touch us less, it will appear much less threatening. We may still feel we have no choice other than to terminate the relationship, but now we will do so without bitterness, free of continuing resentment and free of continuing karmic bondage.

Forgiveness is the greatest gift the inner planet player can give to the other person—and to themselves. When we forgive the outer planet player, we also forgive that part of ourselves reflected in his negative behaviour towards us. By loving the outer planet player sufficiently to make this gesture, we are ultimately loving ourselves. And in loving ourselves we confirm our right to a totally joyful, healthy and abundant future.

The Sun

In the natal chart the Sun represents the urge to make our mark on the world as an individual, to express our creativity and to receive recognition from others. The difficulty or ease with which we attain this directly influences the way we feel about ourselves, for which reason the Sun likewise rules our self-image and the level of our self-esteem. The Sun is also representative of our father as our role model for self-projection and achievement in the outside world.

In chart comparisons, individuals whose outer planets form aspects with our Sun will influence our ability to express ourselves spontaneously, to be true to ourselves and gain acknowledgement of our talents. They will promote or frustrate our creativity, depending upon the nature of the cross-aspect and their own level of enlightenment, and thus will help or hinder us in establishing our identity and fulfilling our unique potential.

Most important, such individuals will exert a strong effect upon our self-esteem. In some cases they will help us to develop pride in ourselves by offering support, praise and encouragement. In others they will challenge our self-confidence by ignoring, criticizing and devaluing our achievements. We may experience such individuals as a source of positive feedback which enables us to maximize our capacity for personal self-expression. Or we may view them as a debilitating influence which undermines our self-image and threatens even to extinguish our very life-force.

In turn, especially where hard aspects are concerned, such individuals are likely to view us as a threat to their own well-being. Frequently it is the manner in which we naturally express ourselves—denoted by the sign placing of our Sun—or our talents, or the recognition we receive from others which triggers a sense of inferiority on their part and unleashes a host of unacknowledged insecurities.

Often we may awaken subconscious memories of a father or father-figure who exposed their weaknesses and caused them pain, sometimes in early childhood or perhaps in a previous incarnation. In either case they are unlikely to perceive us for what we really are, but simply as a projection of their own hidden fears. Something about the way we express ourselves seems to arouse their sense of vulnerability and cause them to seek to protect themselves from the possibility of further pain.

Unless they are able to develop some clear insight into their motivations, the end result is that they are likely to inhibit our free expression of our creativity by overt or subtle opposition and to cause us to feel uncomfortable about being ourselves in their presence.

The Moon

The Moon rules our feeling nature and our expression of those feelings in terms of our habitual reactions, our mannerisms and our general disposition. It symbolizes the most spontaneous aspect of our nature, inasmuch as we have less control over our emotional responses than over our speech or our actions. These responses are inbuilt, having been acquired through our earliest perceptions of the world, in particular our relationship with our mother, long before the development of other functions of our personality.

The Moon symbolizes an instinctive part of ourselves which we can do little to modify or defend and which is thus highly vulnerable. Of itself the Moon has no means of self-protection and is open to outer influences of all kinds, which can affect and alter our mood from one moment to another. The Moon stands for that side of us which is dependent upon a stable, sustaining and

comforting environment for its well-being, which is easily un-
settled and is made anxious by destabilizing or threatening circumstances. Above all it represents our need for nurturing and for
emotional security, a need which may or may not be met fully
depending upon our karmic inheritance.

In the natal chart the Moon and its aspects paint a vivid picture
of our emotional make-up and the way this is affected by the
energies of the outer planets. In chart comparisons also, we can
glean detailed information as to how our emotions are swayed by
other people and how easily we can express our feelings in their
company, depending upon the aspects formed between our Moon
and the outer planets in their chart.

Individuals whose outer planets form angles with our Moon are
liable to pervade the very essence of our being in a way which can
be highly disturbing where challenging aspects are concerned.
Where such individuals direct negative energies towards us, we are
likely to feel threatened at the innermost level, which in turn can
undermine our emotional security, leading eventually to psycho-
somatic illness.

In the case of flowing aspects where mainly positive energies are
concerned, we are more likely to welcome the close emotional
interaction which cross-aspects with such individuals can produce.
This will depend, however, on the natal condition of our Moon
and thus on our basic willingness to open ourselves to others at
the feeling level.

People whose charts contain outer planets in close aspect to our
Moon always make a marked emotional impact upon us. In some
cases they may arouse strong feelings of empathy or excitement on
our part, in others we may feel that they frustrate or ignore our
emotional needs or seek to dominate us at the emotional level.

Where challenging cross-aspects are concerned, such people
seem compelled to adopt tough emotional defence measures to
protect themselves from the threat they perceive us to represent.
Our instinctive reactions and responses, represented by the sign
placing of our Moon, appear to highlight their awareness of the
shortcomings of their own feeling nature, shortcomings which
they now seek to conceal by denying our expression of the
respective feelings.

And if, as often happens, they subconsciously equate us with a
mother-figure who once caused them pain, they may go to any

lengths to gain the emotional upper hand in order to avoid further suffering. It depends upon the outer planet which they embody as to how they will attempt to achieve this emotional control. But whenever they are operating without true self-awareness, their behaviour is likely to lead to the denial of our emotional needs and the creation of acute emotional tension.

Mercury

Mercury, traditionally the messenger of the gods, is interpreted astrologically as the urge to communicate through the spoken or written word and its position in our birth chart determines the ease or lack of ease we experience in this area. The natal placing of Mercury is also descriptive of the nature and quality of our mind and the thought processes we customarily employ to analyse everyday problems.

Mercury rules the means whereby we achieve understanding of the world about us, in part through the instinctive functioning of our brain, in part through the education we undertake to refine our basic intellectual tools. Our approach to learning, the way in which we are able to absorb knowledge, and problems we may face in this respect are also revealed by our natal Mercury. Fundamental comprehension difficulties not only detract from our learning prospects but also disadvantage our human relations, where the misinterpretation of verbal messages can eventually represent a serious source of conflict.

When, in a chart comparison, our Mercury receives stressful aspects from one or more of the other person's outer planets, such misunderstandings are likely to play a major role in the relationship. Commonly we will feel that we can't make ourselves heard by the other person, perhaps because they simply don't listen, or perhaps because they perpetually seek to control the conversation by steering us away from topics they feel uncomfortable with.

The mental vexation we experience in such cases can seriously affect our well-being since we are persistently unable to give voice to feelings urgently in need of an outlet. In the long run we may lose all confidence in our ability for productive verbal exchange, leading us to bite our tongue rather than endure further frustration.

Where flowing cross-aspects are concerned, such communication difficulties are less probable and we are more likely to find a good listener in the other person, someone who is able to interpret our verbal statements accurately and respond to them clearly and helpfully. The ease of communication we can experience with such an individual often provides the foundation for a relationship which thrives in every facet of its whole, since all problems can be effectively thrashed out. By way of contrast, the fundamental inability of two people to discuss important issues honestly can ultimately erode the whole fabric of the relationship, regardless of how healthy it might appear at first sight.

An individual whose outer planets form close aspects with our Mercury exerts a profound effect not only on our verbal self-expression but also on the basic workings of our mind. With positive cross-aspects an outer planet player can help us to restructure our thinking patterns, clear long-standing mental blocks and expand our awareness of the world about us. But in more challenging chart comparisons, the attempts of the outer planet player to reshape our thought processes may be experienced by us as unwelcome and menacing. Repeated criticism or manipulation of our mind can leave us with a mental inferiority complex which deters us from intellectual endeavour, however good our true potential may be.

Outer planet players seem prone to thwart or attack the Mercury player when their perception of him triggers a sense of intellectual inadequacy or a fear of facing some part of their mind which they have carefully sought to suppress. Perhaps it is the Mercury player's sensitivity which strikes such terror in them, or perhaps it is his assertiveness, qualities which they are currently unable to express spontaneously and which they now seek to suppress in the Mercury player.

In some cases the Mercury individual may remind the outer planet player of a past teacher or instructor who initiated their present sense of fear or inferiority. The result is frequently a resurgence of old bitterness which is now transferred onto the Mercury player, to the detriment of both participants in the relationship.

Venus

Without Venus there can be no human interaction nor any

coming together for the purpose of co-operation and mutual pleasure, for this is the planet which rules relationships of all types, whether romantic or platonic. In the birth chart Venus symbolizes our desire to get to know others, to establish harmony with them by ascertaining what we have in common and to experience enjoyment in the pursuit of shared interests.

Primarily this planet is associated with the urge to attract by charm and physical appeal, since such attributes are crucial to our success in relationships, especially at the onset. Once a relationship has been established, however, the spotlight falls more upon recreational pleasures, and common tastes become of greater importance to its prospects than mere physical or sexual attraction.

Also bound up with the significance of Venus is our approach to material assets and to money, since usually this must be expended in order to partake of many pleasures. Where two people differ in their spending habits and possess dissimilar values, considerable strain can be placed on a relationship, particularly when it involves the joint management of finances.

More than any other of the inner planets, when our Venus receives aspects from another person's outer planets, it symbolizes a powerful link with the other individual and an inevitability that we will become involved with them in some way, in certain cases for better and in certain cases for worse.

With positive cross-aspects we are likely to receive clear signals from the other person that they find us attractive, which encourages us to instigate and develop the contact. As the relationship unfolds we may receive beneficial insights from them which help us to maximize our potential to give and receive pleasure in life. Often they will introduce us to new cultural and leisure activities, broadening and deepening our appreciation of beauty and our ability to experience and impart sensual enjoyment. And frequently they can be of assistance to us in purely practical terms by helping us to transform our material values and our handling of resources.

In the case of hard aspects between our Venus and an outer planet in another person's chart, the bond, albeit powerful, is likely to be slightly uneasy and coloured by feelings of love and hate or attraction and repulsion. A common stumbling block is the ambivalence of the outer planet player towards the Venus individual's charms, manifesting as intermittent disapproval of her appearance or dress, perhaps by downright criticism, perhaps by disinterest or lack of attention.

The outer planet player's hostility derives from a sense of inferiority in the face of Venus's overt display of the very qualities in which he feels so inadequate and may also be linked to his unconscious comparison of the Venus player with an antagonistic female from his past. Especially when Venus is a woman, this hostility can be seriously detrimental to her belief in her sexual desirability, leading to loss of confidence, resentment and perhaps to frigidity.

At a deeper level, the attacks of the outer planet player centre upon the Venus player's aesthetic values and are expressed by a subtle condemnation of her tastes. It is precisely what the Venus player finds most appealing and worthy of expenditure that grates so hard against the outer planet player, since these are indulgences that he has denied to himself and finds difficult to accept in the Venus individual.

The money conflicts which inevitably arise in such cross-aspects may ultimately threaten the entire structure of the relationship: they are experienced by the Venus player not simply as a censure of her spending habits but often as a rejection of her core beliefs and values, which strikes at the very heart of her being.

Mars

The very necessary but often misused quality of self-assertion is ruled by the planet Mars. Mars symbolizes our instinct for survival —the urge to claim and seize that which will fulfil our needs, the urge to defend ourselves from potential assailants. In its negative polarity Mars is cruel and merciless in its destruction of anything that obstructs its goals, but when operating positively it can provide us with the courage to stand up for our rights and make an impact on the world despite opposition and criticism.

In the natal chart the position of Mars represents the nature and quality of our will. It describes the things we feel most fervently about, the manner in which we make those feelings felt, and the extent to which we are likely to be successful in our goals. Mars can be considered to symbolize our desire nature and more specifically our libido, providing an accurate picture of what arouses us sexually and what inhibits us.

As in the birth chart, aspects to Mars in a relationship comparison are fundamental to our understanding of core issues, since they throw light on the deep passions which inflame the two individuals and how they give vent to those passions. When an outer planet in another person's chart forms a close aspect with our Mars, they will affect the ease with which we express our strongest feelings, both emotional and sexual. If the aspect is harmonious we may feel encouraged to assert ourselves by that person's presence. But where hard or inharmonious aspects are concerned, we may find it more difficult to be true to ourselves in their company and may conceal, exaggerate or distort our assertiveness due to their influence.

In particular, it is our anger and our sexual drive which are most likely to be modified by another person's outer planet in hard aspect with our Mars. Depending upon the outer planet, these drives may be ignited or quenched, resulting in repeated confrontation or a pattern of aloofness and coldness. Someone's Saturn, for example, in hard aspect with our Mars can seriously inhibit our expression of passionate feelings of all kinds. In a long-term relationship this can result in continuous self-repression with the possibility of eventual physical or psychological dis-ease.

It is our Mars placing which arouses the most profound negative reactions in personal relationships, probably because the other person feels threatened physically by us, rather than simply emotionally or intellectually as is the case with the other inner planets. According to the sign placing of our Mars, our confidence, our strength and our natural assertiveness may trigger a sense of vulnerability on their part, which impels them to adopt the appropriate defence tactics to avoid being overpowered by us. Often, however, the outer planet player's reaction has less to do with us as individuals than our resemblance to a male peer whose influence was detrimental to them in the past and whom they still fear or resent in some way.

When our Mars receives hard aspects not only are we likely to bring out the worst in the outer planet player, but they in turn may bring out the worst in us by activating an angry reaction, either externalized or internalized and representative of a destructive use of our Martian energy. But when an outer planet is functioning harmoniously, its interaction with our Mars can elicit the very best from us by structuring, targeting and empowering our energy drive and helping us to use it to our greatest advantage. It depends on our karma as to whether we are fortunate enough to receive this dynamic support from the other person and whether we have the good sense to accept it.

The Ascendant

Although not strictly an inner planet, the Ascendant is a highly personal feature of our birth chart since its position changes by one degree every four minutes and thus more rapidly than any other component of the horoscope, apart from the Midheaven. For this reason an aspect between our Ascendant and an outer planet in another person's chart is likely to influence us at a more intimate level than any other, and will specifically describe the prime challenge of the relationship.

Standing as it does for our persona, or the mask we adopt in order to relate to the outside world, our Ascendant is the most immediately perceptible facet of our being. As that part of ourselves which we cannot camouflage or conceal, it is powerful in its impact on the other person and in turn is highly vulnerable to their responses towards us. The mutual attraction—or repulsion—is usually instantaneous and ongoing and it is particularly difficult for either person in the relationship to change their instinctive reaction to each other.

When our Ascendant is experienced as threatening by an outer planet player, our personality is liable to represent a continuous source of irritation whenever we are in their company. Because it is perpetually on view, our Ascendant cannot be de-emphasized or merged into the background, as can certain of the inner planets. When there is conflict between ourselves and an outer planet player, our presence may have the effect of a red flag held permanently before a bull. But equally, in the case of a harmonious cross-aspect, he is likely to experience our presence as a constant source of excitement and delight.

Cross-aspects to our Ascendant are associated with predominantly physical attractions, since it is our bodily appearance—as opposed to our mind or our feelings—which has such a strong effect on the outer planet player, reflecting a hidden facet of his own psyche. The impact we make on the other person is so powerful because it is based on virtually everything about us, including our speech, our mannerisms, our dress and entire style of self-presentation.

Where the outer planet player is comfortable with that part of himself which he perceives in us, he is likely to be positively attracted by us and to appreciate us as a mirror image of himself. But where the outer planet player is fearful and distrustful of that side of himself which we represent, the attraction may be tainted by a sense of wariness and an urgent desire to control us in the same way that he controls what we symbolize in himself.

Cross-aspects to our Ascendant are associated with the longest-lasting of relationships. Harmonious planetary links can produce an attraction which never dies and which results in a lifetime of mutual stimulation. Challenging cross-aspects, however, can give rise to interminable stress which is manifestly detrimental to our well-being but from which we feel unable to release ourselves. Even in the most difficult of relationships, the physical attraction is often too great for the two people to let each other go.

Relationships of this intensity inevitably have a powerful effect on our self-image, which may be to our detriment or our benefit depending upon our karmic history with the other person. An outer planet player's appreciation of our personality and appearance can serve as an ongoing ego-booster, which helps us to achieve all our goals. But his persistent disapproval or criticism can be highly demoralizing, giving us the sense that there is something wrong with us, that we aren't 'good enough' as we are.

When an outer planet player is unable to handle that part of himself which he perceives in us, he is liable to make persistent attempts to change the way we act or the way we look, as symbolized by our Ascendant sign. If his emotional hold over us is strong, we may do our utmost to comply with these demands, often drastically changing our appearance or behaviour simply to avoid the risk of losing him. Such self-betrayal may well ease the discomfort the outer planet player experiences in our company, but it can seriously inhibit our personal development since we are abandoning our true identity and life's purpose.

However much we imagine we need another person in our life, if we must become someone different in order to win his affection, we would ultimately be better off without him. And however much he may profess to love us, unless he can accept and value us precisely as we are, his love is shallow and without foundation.

Only when the outer planet player has come to terms with and released his subconscious fear of us, is he able to express true love for us. Only when he has acquired real respect for our Ascendant sign is he capable of enhancing our personality without attempting to modify it to his own ends.

Cross-aspects between our Ascendant and another person's outer planets often involve a tough but ultimately worthwhile struggle. When the positive polarity of an outer planet connects harmoniously with our Ascendant, its influence is unsurpassed in bringing out the best in us by making us feel good about being exactly who and what we are—without apologies and with no strings attached.

JUPITER, KARMA AND CROSS-ASPECTS

Jupiter is not generally considered a 'karmic' planet, since the word karma is normally associated only with painful experiences and even at its worst Jupiter is relatively harmless in its manifestation. But if we interpret karma as both challenging and harmonious experience, Jupiter can be recognized as an important karmic influence, correlating mainly with the fortunate outcome of positive thoughts, feelings and actions but also linked with the less than fortunate consequences of over-confidence, over-optimism and over-expansion.

Because its more challenging effects are hardly in the same league as the psychological trauma engendered by Saturn, Uranus, Neptune and Pluto, Jupiter cannot be strictly classified as an outer planet, yet neither does it come under the heading of an inner planet, since it does not represent a facet of the ego.

The planet Jupiter in the natal chart is a symbol of group consciousness ruling our faith and beliefs, our moral codes and our need to abide by defined laws of living. In aspect with the inner planets it reflects, in our individual self-expression, the moral and religious conditioning inculcated during childhood and previous lives. When it is aspected by outer planets, it challenges us to question and transform our philosophy of life on the basis of personal insights and inspiration.

At the highest level Jupiter challenges us to move beyond blind self-belief and false optimism towards an understanding of universal law and the principle of cause and effect. It teaches us that wealth and happiness are acquired not by taking but by giving, in that generosity is a powerful generator of personal abundance. In helping us to arrive at this awareness, Jupiter compels us to confront issues relating to our judgement and may oblige us to suffer the consequences of over-assurance, extravagance and foolish gambles. The difficulties which arise for us under the influence of Jupiter are thus essentially self-created, unlike the challenges of Saturn, Uranus, Neptune and Pluto, which often arise from outside of ourselves and over which we may have no control.

When an inner planet in our chart is aspected by another person's Jupiter, we will tend to absorb his level of attunement to that planet. When we live in close proximity to the Jupiter player we cannot fail but be influenced by his belief system and moral values, which may lead us towards a more enlightened outlook or cause us to over-extend ourselves, depending on our karmic account.

Jupiter cross-aspects are always connected with high-spirited, mirth-filled, mutually benevolent interrelationships, hence their reputation as highly desirable. But it depends upon the spiritual level at which the Jupiter individual is functioning as to what lies at the source of the light-heartedness and laughter.

When the Jupiter player possesses a soundly based faith, he will help us develop the refined sense of humour associated with understanding of the law of cause and effect. He will instil us with the true sense of optimism which arises from the realization that our good fortune rests entirely in our own hands.

But when the Jupiter player has little self-awareness or understanding of universal law, his expression of humour is likely to be shallow, sometimes cruelly directed at the afflictions of others, and will do little to gladden our soul. When the Jupiter player is reliant solely on 'luck' for his prosperity and happiness, he may instil us with false optimism which leads us into errors of judgement and the depletion of our resources. And when the Jupiter player is blind to the system of spiritual fair play constantly at work in our lives, he may incite us to waste energy fighting for ill-founded causes through an unwarranted sense of injustice.

When we meet with our own ill-developed Jupiter in a karmic relationship with someone whose Jupiter closely aspects our chart, we must witness at first hand the unhappy results of lack of limit-ation. Apart from the obvious material stresses of the effects of over-spending, we may also suffer from the Jupiter player's tendency to make promises without the wherewithal to carry them through, to expect too much from us or to take us continuously for granted. Negative Jupiter functions with an almost total absence of sensitivity, being far too absorbed in his over-expansive, get-rich-quick schemes to pay attention to our emotional needs.

But despite the sense of neglect, impatience or sheer exasperation we may experience towards the Jupiter player, it is difficult for us to remain angry for long at his foolish blunders and well-meaning incompetence. It is hard for us to resist his unquenchable spirit of merriment which can continue to attract and delight us even in the most testing of relationships. It is for this reason that Jupiter cross-aspects are in themselves rarely responsible for bitter partings, even in the case of the worst Jupiterian behaviour. And it is also for this reason that Jupiter relationships are rarely considered to be linked with really hard karma, although the karmic lesson is certainly there to be learned.

Jupiter–Ascendant cross-aspects count among the most covetable in any relationship, inasmuch as the personality of the Ascendant player stimulates the Jupiter player's joviality and largesse in such a way that he is able to lift the spirits of the Ascendant player and bring positive vibrations into his life. However, it is not a contact which makes for diligence or practical accomplishment, and in some cases each may encourage the other towards idleness and excessive frivolity.

When Jupiter in one chart aspects the Sun in another, Jupiter is likely to instil the Sun player with confidence to develop his self-expression in the area of life ruled by the Sun's sign placing and to give generously of himself without necessarily seeking material gain. But when functioning disharmoniously Jupiter may over-inflate the Sun's pride and ambitions to such an extent that the Sun attempts projects beyond his capabilities and resources with resultant failure and humiliation.

Jupiter in cross-aspect to the Moon exudes a delightfully cheering influence capable of dispelling the Moon's moods and depression with a humorous and philosophical view-point. But where the Moon is itself ebullient by nature, Jupiter may have an over-stimulating effect, magnifying her excitability and inciting her towards rash actions. And not uncommonly Jupiter may be insensitive to the Moon's more profound psychological needs, trampling on her feelings and taking her devotion for granted.

Jupiter–Mercury is an essentially loquacious cross-aspect in which each individual may vie continuously with the other for verbal supremacy. Where Mercury tends towards reserve or taciturnity, Jupiter can develop his communications skills, and where Mercury has low intellectual self-esteem Jupiter can build his self-assurance. Jupiter can usually help Mercury to see any situation in a positive light and to understand the philosophical basis of any challenge. Problems arise only when Jupiter over-extends Mercury's mental self-confidence, urging him towards over-optimism, impractical schemes and the occasional serious error of judgement.

A cross-aspect between Jupiter and Venus can provide Venus with the impetus to develop her artistic and creative talents and to make the most of her looks and charm. Jupiter can also exert an expansive influence on Venus's social life, introducing her to beneficent friends and contacts, but by the same token he can also prove a dissipative influence on her physical and financial resources. Not least, Jupiter's encouragement towards high living and over-indulgence can have a disastrous effect on Venus's looks, causing her to lose her beauty well ahead of her time.

In cross-aspect with Mars, Jupiter can have a tremendous energy-boosting influence which sparks off Mars's enthusiasm and adrenalin flow. Although clearly of positive help to a weak or lethargic Mars, where Mars is inherently strong this can over-magnify his aggression and push him into potentially dangerous situations. Mars in turn is likely to stimulate Jupiter's high spirits and joviality, resulting in much tomfoolery and horseplay but often very little in the way of concrete achievement or material advancement. At best, however, each can encourage the other to give generously of their physical resources through nobility of spirit and to pursue goals with the highest moral motivation.

When Jupiter in one chart is aspected by an outer planet in the other, the first player will be challenged to reassess his beliefs and moral values as a result of the other's catalytic influence. In the case of Saturn, the practicality of Jupiter's philosophy is likely to be tested and if necessary restructured and any over-expansiveness may be harshly criticized and subjected to restriction. Uranus exerts a strongly stimulating effect on Jupiter, encouraging him to break free from early moral indoctrination and childhood belief systems and to formulate his own individual life philosophy and values. Neptune will often help to spiritualize Jupiter's outlook, elevate his ideals and help him to channel his generosity of spirit into altruistic outlets. But Pluto can have the profoundest and most dramatic influence on Jupiter, cruelly exposing the unsoundness and emptiness of his dearest-held beliefs and aspirations and often triggering a total transformation in his attitude towards life.

Transits of Jupiter to any cross-aspect are likely to coincide with a sudden flaring up of energy which forces into the open any dormant conflicts relating to the planets under transit. Jupiter has the effect of dramatizing a relationship issue, or rendering it larger than life in a way that enables it to be fully experienced and properly understood. If we enjoy excitement, respond well to crisis and do not cringe from facing issues square on, we are likely to thrive on transits of Jupiter which frequently provide the opportunity for change of a spectacular nature within a relationship.

The manner in which we handle that opportunity depends principally upon our level of attunement to Jupiter and the soundness of our philosophy of life. Where we possess strong spiritual ideals or moral values, we can call on these to settle our differences amicably and survive the storm with dignity. Where we possess an instinctive generosity of spirit, we are usually prepared to give unstintingly of ourselves to sort out the mutual difficulties in the relationship.

But where we rely merely on blind self-confidence, we may push our luck just once too often and precipitate the final break-up of a relationship which has long been tottering on the brink. It is in cases such as these that Jupiter, 'the great benefic', is deserving of its incongruous reputation for causing trials and tribulations in transit. Jupiter transits serve primarily to test our wisdom, and where this is lacking to any substantial extent they are liable to make us look extremely foolish.

THE TRANSITS OF THE OUTER PLANETS AND PERSONAL RELATIONSHIPS

The transits of the outer planets to cross-aspected planets in chart comparisons coincide with the unfolding of important relationship challenges, when long-standing problems, often dating back from past lives, are likely to recur and must be dealt with. These are the times when two people may fall prey to feelings of mutual disinterest, mistrust or bitterness which erect an insurmountable barrier between them. Or they may use such times to deepen and expand their love for one another, elevating the relationship onto a new and higher level of consciousness.

The closer the cross-aspect, the more likely are the two individuals to be influenced simultaneously by the transiting planet, which can exert a more powerfully healing effect on the relationship than if the two people were influenced by the transit at different times. A precise cross-aspect under transit offers them the opportunity to undergo concurrent self-change and to move forward in unison in their spiritual development. By way of contrast, when our partner changes profoundly in some way but we do not, we may fear that he is moving away from us or becoming someone whom we no longer understand.

Transits of an outer planet to two inner planets in conjunction by cross-aspect will highlight the similarities between the two people which can help them to embark on new projects in a spirit of harmony and co-operation, but might also emphasize common negative tendencies, leading to deadlock.

Transits to inner planets in opposition or square by cross-aspect allow the two people to draw on contrasting or complementary qualities which can help them to work together more efficiently. But frequently they will also bring to the fore fundamental differences which may not previously have been particularly notice-able. For example, the contrasting approach of one person with Moon in Aries and another with Mars in Capricorn may become so exaggerated and entrenched under a Pluto transit that the whole fabric of the relationship will be threatened unless they can reach some kind of compromise.

Outer planet transits to a cross-aspect between an inner planet in one chart and an outer planet in another mark the timing of major karmic issues and often coincide with events or develop-ments which will bring a festering conflict to a head. Grievances previously kept hidden may now be forced out into the open, and the two players face the choice of re-enacting or breaking the karmic pattern which has bonded them to one another lifetime after lifetime.

In that each can do no more than highlight the fundamental challenge represented by a cross-aspect, the transits of all the outer planets are similar in effect. For example, a transit of Uranus cannot change the inherently sombre character of a Moon–Saturn cross-aspect, but it can enable the two people to gain sufficient detachment from one another to reassess their inhibited emotional interaction with greater understanding.

Each outer planet has the potential to throw fresh light on an issue, allowing the two people to consider their difficulties from a new angle. Indeed it is only when a cross-aspect has received a series of outer planet transits that a relationship may begin to be healed. It is the transits of Pluto which allow for the greatest breakthroughs in relationship problems, although Saturn, Uranus and Neptune each have their own part to play in permitting release from interpersonal conflicts.

Transits of Saturn

Transits of Saturn to cross-chart aspects provide the two indivi-duals with the opportunity to take a serious look at their relation-ship and decide where it should go from now. Saturn transits often mark the reaching of a crossroads, when the two people affirm or renew their commitment to one another or decide that they no longer owe each other any commitment and therefore begin to move apart.

The function of Saturn transits is to allow us to achieve a more balanced expression of responsibility, cutting back on obligations where these have become too onerous, or taking on new duties when we have the capacity and desire to do so. Within a relationship, transiting Saturn may challenge one or both people to assume a role which involves additional responsibility, for example by marrying or starting a family, or perhaps taking on the care of a sick child or spouse.

But the transits of this planet can also coincide with the realization that there is nothing more of a helpful nature that one person can do for the other and that the usefulness of the relationship to both individuals is coming to an end. These are the times when a long-suffering wife may finally walk out on an insensitive or brutish husband, or an exasperated parent may at last eject sponging grown-up offspring.

Saturn transits are particularly important from the spiritual standpoint in that they allow us clear insight into the current state of our karmic account. It is not uncommon to experience an overwhelming and inexplicable conviction that we must now take on a particularly demanding karmic task which we would otherwise find unthinkable. Alternatively we may experience a powerful intuition at such times that we have paid our karmic debt to another person and can free ourselves from our self-imposed bondage. Subconsciously we all have the ability to sense when our dues have been paid and the time for release has arrived. It is by no means necessary to do penance for a lifetime on account of one karmic debt.

The misery and alienation sometimes linked to Saturn transits can result from an inability to get in touch with our intuition or to accept that we have paid our dues. Those of us who lack the art of self-forgiveness or whose sense of responsibility is over-developed can find ourselves driven by a self-destructive force at the times of such transits. In some cases we may feel compelled to continue with an empty and often detrimental marriage with grim and tight-lipped determination in the belief that we must do our duty, no matter what the personal consequences. In others we may continue to allow ourselves to be exploited by over-demanding children or colleagues in the belief that exploitation and suffering are our just fate.

A typical problem in Saturn transits is that of communication breakdown, with one or both individuals lacking the ability to take a realistic look at the relationship and to thrash out the underlying problems. Personal embarrassment and fear of offending propriety are the classic Saturnian inhibitors which deter us from bringing our grievances out into the open. We dread the socially humiliating consequences of washing our dirty linen in public and prefer to accept the emotionally devastating consequences of keeping our pain to ourselves.

Transits of Saturn always enhance our fear of failure or rejection and often cause us to raise our defence barriers as a means of self-protection. Two people with a cross-aspect transited by Saturn can experience a seemingly unbridgeable gulf between each other at such times which effectively prevents any honest communication. Yet it is precisely on the occasion of Saturn transits that really clear and honest exchange is needed if a relationship is to be placed on a healthy footing capable of withstanding the next cycle of Saturn.

In romantic partnerships the distance which customarily arises between two people during transits of Saturn inevitably influences their sexual relationship, in some cases leading to a total discontinuation of sexual communication. It is especially in the case of close cross-aspects that this problem can occur, since the two partners are held back simultaneously by Saturnian inhibitions, making it very hard for them to break through the sexual impasse.

The verbal and/or sexual communication breakdown frequently associated with Saturn transits often leads to an exacerbation of existing problems, since issues which are repressed or ignored inevitably become magnified out of all proportion to their true significance.

But perhaps our greatest challenge, when faced with transits of Saturn to cross-aspects, is to make a conscious effort to counter the social anxieties to which we become prone at such times and which can wreak havoc in relationships of all kinds if left unchecked. It is only too easy to turn into a nag or a slave-driver and to lose all sense of fun in the desire to see the fulfilment of some social aspiration, either through our own efforts or the efforts of our partner or child. Preoccupation with status and worldly achievement during transits of Saturn can ultimately freeze any genuine love and sensitivity between the two people concerned.

The pragmatic outlook predominant during such transits can be useful, however, in sorting out the practical details of relationship issues, especially when contracts must be drawn up, for example on the occasion of marriages, divorces or business partnerships. It can also be useful in deciding upon the practical steps required to tackle a source of conflict within a relationship, whether of an emotional, sexual or financial nature, and perhaps to obtain professional advice and guidance.

It may well be very difficult to solve our relationship difficulties completely under Saturn transits, but what we can do is to stand back and survey them in the cold light of day, to decide how much effort we should channel into their solution and to initiate the appropriate remedial action.

Saturn transits are the time for laying our cards on the table, for making tough deals, not only with others but also with ourselves. It isn't agreeable to come to a decision that a relationship is over, but sometimes this is necessary when Saturn dispels our delusions and strips everything bare. It isn't easy to come to the realization that demanding work is called for in a relationship, if we are to fulfil the sense of obligation that can also hit us so profoundly at these times.

We must be extremely hard on ourselves and perhaps also on others in order to implement such decisions effectively. Yet the make-or-break crises associated with transits of Saturn represent vitally important turning-points in our emotional and social life. And their function is to take us step by step closer to release from karmic bondage and the attainment of true spiritual freedom.

Transits of Uranus

Uranus transits have a reputation for making things happen to people, however hard they may try to resist change or shield themselves from its influence. Indeed, there can be no avoiding the influence of this planet, since its function is to trigger the main karmic challenges in our life which in turn are likely to result in a sudden change of course for us.

Whereas transits of Saturn prepare us to take on a karmic burden and transits of Neptune and Pluto help us to mop up the after-effects, it is when Uranus hits a cross-aspect that the karmic issue between two people will burst into manifestation and will have to be dealt with in practical terms. There is rarely any time to plan or reflect during a transit of Uranus—we must act on our intuition to handle the immediate crisis and to adapt to the unexpected change in circumstances.

It often seems that there is nowhere to run when this planet strikes, obliging us to confront relationship problems that previously we may have brushed under the carpet but which are now blasted into manifestation. Neptunian deceptions will suddenly be unmasked, subtle Plutonic manipulation will now appear crude and blatant, and insidious Saturnian criticism will take on a more threatening note. In transit Uranus tends to act as a catalyst, electrifying the effects of other planets which now are experienced more vividly and intensely.

When we play an outer planet in a cross-aspect, a transit of Uranus will shatter most of our inhibitions in expressing the essence of the outer planet, and where our tendency is to express the negative characteristics of the outer planet we may now do so with newfound disregard for convention or decency. A previously controlled urge to cheat or to bully may now become uncontainable and lead to a crisis in a relationship which had seemingly been trouble-free.

When we play an inner planet in a cross-aspect transited by Uranus, our perception level rises whilst our tolerance level falls, making us more aware of the destructive behaviour of the other person but less willing to put up with it, however much we love them. The self-preservation instinct which is often felt during Uranus transits leads to many sudden endings in relationships.

What often seems to happen during transits of Uranus is that the two people are able to put some emotional distance between them, achieve some detachment and perhaps develop a greater degree of personal independence. In the case of cross-aspects which involve over-dependency or over-attachment, this sudden sense of freedom can be highly beneficial, helping Saturn-bound individuals to free themselves from their rut and Pluto-bound people to give each other a little more space. Generally this process is more difficult for one of the individuals than the other, usually the one whose chart contains the greater fixity in terms of signs or planetary aspects.

In a romantic relationship, the partner with the greatest resistance to change may often feel seriously threatened by the libertine behaviour which can occur in the other person as a result of a Uranus transit and which frequently leads to a flirtation or affair and to the subsequent disruption of the partnership.

The situation can be easier to cope with if the two partners are influenced simultaneously by Uranus's liberating vibrations and are thus likely to sow their wild oats in unison. It is for this reason that tight links between charts can be healthier for a relationship than wide-orbed cross-aspects, which result in a time-lag of a couple of years between outer planet transits of the one chart and the other. People may find they can ride a crisis more successfully if they are experiencing the same kind of emotions at the same time and thus have a better understanding of, and more empathy with, the other's moods, attitude and behaviour.

Nevertheless, in any kind of relationship, one of the individuals inevitably feels less comfortable than the other with the new element of freedom which manifests during a Uranus transit. Our instinctive reaction when we fear we may be losing someone we care deeply for, perhaps a lover, perhaps a teenage son or daughter, is to attempt to hold onto them by restricting their freedom. But this approach is doomed to failure where transits of Uranus are concerned: any form of restraint is anathema to this planet and those influenced by its rays will brook no denial in seizing their independence by whatever means proves necessary.

It is perhaps the greatest strength and the greatest hazard of Uranus transits that they allow two people to move away from one another and to obtain some mutual detachment. This 'distancing' differs from that which occurs during Saturn transits in that in the case of Saturn we are motivated by a fear of rejection but in the case of Uranus by a fear of commitment.

Certainly it can be beneficial for two people to give each other space to develop their individuality and independence, when this happens within the framework of a loving, supportive and committed relationship. But the permanence of a relationship can be placed at risk during Uranus transits if the two people create too wide a gap between each other which subsequently proves unbridgeable. This is especially the case in romantic partnerships, where a short period of indulgence in sexual freedom can have serious long-term consequences for the stability of the relationship.

The desire for sexual experimentation is but one manifestation of the deep-seated urge to try out new types of behaviour which we customarily experience during transits of Uranus. Uranus transits are primarily about making choices and exercising our free will. They give us the opportunity to find a new approach to the karmic problems which come to the fore and demand our attention at such times. These are also the times when we can draw on our intuition to gain flashes of insight into the core issues between ourselves and others and how best we can handle them.

Change is always an integral part of Uranus transits and it simply cannot be ignored. We must be prepared for the safe, familiar pattern of our relationship to be disrupted by sudden karmic challenges which call upon all our ingenuity and adaptability. However long we have known someone, we should never feel it is too late to learn something new from the relationship. Indeed, it is precisely when we are resting smugly on our laurels, when we believe that nothing could disrupt the perfect harmony of a partnership, that Uranus is likely to deliver us with a huge and unwelcome surprise.

Transits of Neptune

Compared to the dramatic events associated with Uranus transits, often very little actually happens when Neptune hits a cross-aspect between two charts. Nevertheless, this planet can produce a marked change of attitude in one or both of the individuals, which is likely to generate a good deal of stress in the relationship.

Transits of Neptune tend to coincide with the karmic aftermath of a relationship trauma. They reflect all the pain, disillusionment and despair we experience when someone we idolized has departed from our life, appears to have let us down or has betrayed our trust. This process of grieving for our lost ideals can continue for a couple of years as Neptune moves back and forth over a sensitive feature of our chart.

When this chart feature is linked by tight aspect to a planet in the chart of another person, the transit of Neptune can trigger a process of mutual disenchantment in which both people become aware that the other is not the person they originally believed him to be. At the same time one or both of the individuals may seek a new outlet for his shattered dreams, perhaps through a romantic infatuation or some other form of escape. The set-up is far from conducive towards harmonious relations, and indeed Neptune can subtly and insidiously undermine any relationship which is based on false hopes and expectations.

As with Saturn, a transit of Neptune to a cross-aspect can lead to a serious communication breakdown as the two individuals retreat into a private world of their own. When this happens, each may silently complain that the other is unable to relate to his feelings or to offer any empathy or understanding. He may fantasize about the perfect partner or parent who would fulfil his every need, who would make everything in his life fine again, but who does not exist except in his own imagination.

It seems that Neptune often drains us of the physical energy to articulate our grievances and the will to try to find a solution. We are emasculated by a sense of futility which convinces us there is nothing we can do about our lot and that all effort is largely wasted. As a consequence of this lethargy, two people can withhold vital feedback from each other which could dramatically transform their emotional or sexual relationship. Even when they do attempt to communicate their feelings, the end result can be confused and misleading, which only adds to the mutual sense of bewilderment and despair.

Unless it can be given some creative outlet, the imagination tends to run wild during transits of Neptune and invariably it is not so much what is actually wrong in a relationship but what we fear may be wrong that causes us anguish. The vagueness, dreaminess and unreliability typical of a partner undergoing a Neptune transit can conspire to convince us that he no longer cares for us or is having an affair. We may also be disturbed by his tendency to get his facts wrong or to indulge in white lies. When it seems we can no longer obtain a straight answer from a previously honest and plain-talking partner, we cannot be blamed for supposing that he is slipping away from us.

In some cases the absent-mindedness may indeed be linked to an affair of the heart but more often than not it is just a symptom of the 'spacing out' which many people experience under a Neptune transit and which has no sinister motive or outcome. Transits of Neptune can be associated with a marked development of the psychic faculties, manifesting as a sudden flowering of intuition, inspiration and extra-sensory perception. When Neptune transits over a cross-aspect between two individuals, they may find that they are able to develop these faculties in unison, which can provide much-needed help in bringing them together. Although

Neptune often has a destructive influence on verbal communication, it encourages a psychic interaction which allows for far greater sensitivity than mere words can achieve.

Two people in a close relationship often find during transits of Neptune that they are able to pick up each other's thoughts even when they are not in each other's company. This serves to build a sense of at-oneness which can deepen their spiritual love for each other and it counteracts the gulf which can drive people apart when a Neptune transit dissolves the desire for physical closeness.

Many people find that their sex-life slows down considerably or even shudders to a halt during transits of Neptune, as their interest moves away from the physical plane towards more etheric or spiritual concepts. In some cases we may find that the gratification we experience at such times through mystical activities such as meditation replaces any desire for sex. In others we may simply be lacking in the physical energy required for fulfilling love-making. But this said, sex can sometimes become very special indeed under transits of Neptune, meeting all the promises held out in romantic fiction.

Neptune always leads us in search of the peak experience—the ultimate high which will fulfil our deepest yearnings. When Neptune transits a cross-aspect it can be fun for the two people to embark on this search together, taking time to enjoy music, art or the theatre in each other's company. The joint practice of meditation is one of the best activities for two people undergoing a simultaneous Neptune transit. The experience of sitting quietly together can open up a whole new level of consciousness in the relationship, allowing a previously undiscovered degree of closeness.

One never really knows how a transit of Neptune is likely to influence two people. It can strengthen and refine the bond between them, elevating their relationship onto a higher, more spiritually fulfilling plane. Alternatively it can distort and poison their interaction, replacing previous affection with a mutual sense of disillusionment and betrayal.

In the final analysis, the way in which we experience Neptune and the way in which it will influence our relationships depends upon the soundness of our ideals. If we have false gods—if we idolize those we love and harbour unrealistic expectations of them or ourselves—we must experience a severe sense of let-down when our rose-coloured spectacles change their hue. But if we place our faith not in human beings but in love itself and in the power of love to overcome all pain, we will find it a good deal easier to weather the disappointments of Neptune transits, to accept the other person as he really is, and to continue to care for him despite everything.

Transits of Neptune challenge us to love others and ourselves, warts and all, a process which requires a good deal of soul-searching and perhaps more than a little private anguish. But at the end of the day the passage of this planet over a cross-aspect can set a karmic relationship on a totally new footing. Its healing vibrations can engender a spirit of selflessness in which personal concerns are placed on one side in the interests of true love.

Transits of Pluto

People do some terrible things to each other under the influence of Pluto transits. Parents can systematically crush a child's spirit in the attempt to exert their authority over him. Husbands or wives can set out to prove their dominance by ruthlessly destroying the partner they once vowed they would love for eternity. We are prone to manifest our cruellest traits at such times and often love would appear to fly completely out of the window. Yet it *is* love, albeit in grossly distorted garb, that drives people on during transits of Pluto to callous and shameful behaviour.

When Pluto transits a cross-aspect between the charts of two individuals, they frequently experience an intensification of their love feelings, which at best is hard to deal with and at worst can be positively overwhelming. The essentially benign emotion called love can mutate at such times into a voracious craving for psychological and perhaps physical control of another person. Blindly, we may convince ourselves that we are motivated by a deep and powerful affection, but in reality we care nothing for the other person's well-being and are concerned only with preventing the loss of an individual on whom we are emotionally dependent.

Jealousy is by far the most common problem we are faced with during transits of Pluto, although recognizing and defining that emotion is often extremely difficult. Mostly we are aware only of the deep anxiety and emotional churning which shatters our previous contentment and which we may blame on a change of behaviour on the part of the loved one. It takes quite a while to realize that the pain we experience at such times generally has no concrete origin and arises simply from our own insecurities. The jealousy which can mar our relationships during Pluto transits has its roots in an upsurgence into our conscious minds of a deep-seated fear of abandonment and a sense of our own unworthiness to inspire and retain love.

When Pluto hits a tight cross-aspect between two people, it is likely to arouse simultaneous feelings of jealousy and insecurity and the characteristic Plutonic urge to seize and maintain control of the loved one. This makes for a potentially explosive situation and unless both individuals are in close touch with their emotions and with the dynamics of their interaction, Pluto can set the scene for a protracted and embittered power battle which rarely has a happy ending. The most acrimonious of divorces are conducted under the influence of Pluto transits which seem to bring out a compulsive desire in both persons to inflict maximum punishment on the other, no matter how much suffering this causes to themselves or their children. We seem hell-bent at such times on wreaking our revenge on the person we believe responsible for our emotional pain and for destroying our happiness and security.

What we invariably fail to realize during a Pluto transit is that we and we alone are responsible for the feelings of jealousy and bitterness which can affect any relationship when this planet points its finger at us. No matter how unreasonably the other person acts towards us, we need not become defenceless victims, we need not accept his negativity. We may not possess the power to change his attitude or behaviour towards us, but we do possess the power to create our own reality.

But Pluto transits are by no means all doom and gloom and many couples are prepared to use these periods to embark on a process of self-awareness and self-change, preferably within the framework of counselling or psychotherapy. Within this set-up it is possible for the two individuals to explore their negative feelings towards one another, so as to gain valuable insights into their interpersonal behaviour patterns.

Many people find that they are able, during these transits, to give each other truthful feedback for the very first time. Others find they can give voice to grievances which have irked them for some time but which have hitherto remained unspoken. Often these are fundamental issues of contention of which neither person has been consciously aware, but which have undermined the well-being of the relationship for a period of many years. The plain talking which must take place during these confrontations can be threatening and painful to both people, but it is a vital element of the process of healing which is the highest manifestation of a Pluto transit. Only by bringing our anxieties and grudges into the open are we able to let go of them and begin the relationship on a new footing.

A Pluto transit to a cross-aspect signals a time for long and intense discussion, a time for probing into the deepest regions of our psyche, which can be both emotionally and physically exhausting. For this reason a transit of Pluto can often work best when the cross-aspect has close orbs and the two people are affected simultaneously by its influence, allowing them greater understanding for each other and the opportunity to work together in a co-counselling situation. But in other cases the emotional demands on two people attempting to 'process their stuff' at the same time can be simply too much and the healing potential is greater when there is a gap of a couple of years between Pluto's transit of the one chart and the other.

Transits of Pluto to parent/child cross-aspects are perhaps hardest to deal with, since for many the idea that a mother or father may harbour feelings of bitterness or jealousy towards their own offspring is unthinkable. Yet Pluto in transit is liable to activate such emotions powerfully, especially between parents and children of the same sex.

It is common for a parent to view his child at such times as a rival for the love of his partner or as a threat to his sense of security, feelings which may be extremely difficult to articulate. But because children need encouragement to express the resentment which they too experience during Pluto transits, it is helpful for the parent to take the lead in honestly describing his own feelings. Frank parent–child dialogue at such times helps to create the basis for a healthy and vibrant relationship capable of withstanding the test of time.

Parents are often held back from honest discussion with their children through fear that by disclosing their vulnerability they may undermine their authority. The need to affirm one's control, both to oneself and to others, is certainly a major theme of Pluto transits, which inhibits our release of negative feelings and leads to manipulative attempts to possess the ones we love. In parent–child cross-aspects a child may feel during a Pluto transit that the grown-up invades his space, both physical and emotional, leaving him no privacy and prying into thoughts and feelings which he does not wish to share. Or a mother may feel at such times that she doesn't have a moment to herself, that her child's needs have come to pervade her entire existence and that she has ceased to function as a person in her own right.

Between lovers the possessiveness characteristic of Pluto transits can have an insidiously destructive influence on their sexual relationship, if one partner begins to feel suffocated or imprisoned by the intensity of the other's demands. This intensity is always discernible during Pluto transits, perhaps simply through subtly aggressive body language experienced by the other person as invasive or menacing. But when two people are committed to developing their self-awareness, they will find it easier to understand each other's possessiveness as reflective of the deep insecurities which surface during Pluto transits and which need to be worked through to heal the relationship.

In terms of karma, transits of Pluto provide the opportunity to wipe the slate clean by severing our bondage to another person. But this release can take place only when we are genuinely able to let go of all feelings of attachment, both negative and positive, which are replaced by a love which is non-possessive and unconditional, the kind of love we are challenged to discover during Pluto transits through a long and often painful journey of self-exploration.

We should be prepared, during Pluto transits, for some ugly behaviour on our own part and on the part of our loved ones. Pluto requires that we face our darkness and bring it into the light for the process of transmutation to unfold. When Pluto transits over a cross-aspect, the two individuals are challenged to witness and assist in each other's regeneration: each is challenged to assume the role of spiritual midwife to the other's emotional and psychological rebirth.

THE KARMIC
CROSS-ASPECTS

The most important karmic issues in a relationship are symbolized by cross-aspects between Saturn, Uranus, Neptune or Pluto on the one hand and the Ascendant, Sun, Moon, Mercury, Venus or Mars on the other. Cross-aspects between inner planets simply indicate basic personality contrasts, which can certainly impose stress on a relationship but which are of karmic significance only if they are additionally aspected by an outer planet in one chart or the other.

Cross-aspects involving the Ascendant of one of the individuals and an outer planet of the other are the most powerful of all the karmic aspects. The Ascendant individual is likely to make an immediate impact on the outer planet player who perceives, in the physical appearance of the Ascendant individual, a part of his own psyche with which he is probably not consciously in touch. Although the same process of attraction unfolds in the case of cross-aspects of an outer planet in one chart to any of the inner planets in the other chart, it is unlikely to be experienced with the same immediacy and constancy as cross-aspects involving the Ascendant.

Of the various types of cross-aspect, the conjunction is by far the most significant since the two individuals identify with each other very closely on the basis of a specific zodiac sign. Oppositions, squares and trines are also of significance in that order and indicate a mutual identification between two people in terms of a specific polarity, quality or element.

A standard orb of 8° works well for cross-conjunctions, cross-oppositions and cross-squares, but most astrologers prefer to reduce the orb to 4° or 5° for cross-trines.

In the following descriptions a theoretical analysis is followed by a real-life case illustrating the practical manifestation of the planetary energies.

THE KARMIC CROSS-ASPECTS OF SATURN

Saturn–Ascendant

Although relationships governed by Saturn cross-aspects usually develop at a slower pace than those involving the other outer planets, a Saturn–Ascendant cross-aspect often results in a physical attraction on the part of Saturn towards the Ascendant player as early as the very first meeting. It is just that it may take Saturn some time to acknowledge that attraction or to do anything about it.

For Saturn it can be something of a revelation to witness the overt expression in the Ascendant player of the very qualities he would most like to possess, although he may never have admitted this even to himself. There before him, in the appearance, speech and mannerisms of the Ascendant player, is his *alter ego*, the personality he assumes in his fantasies, the role model he secretly aspires to. Especially in the case of the conjunction, Saturn can experience an instant and powerful admiration for a specific quality in the Ascendant player which he feels to be lacking in himself.

The Ascendant player is likely to be struck by a mutual sense of admiration for Saturn whom she may perceive as a protective figure to whom she can turn for practical help and guidance and who will provide her with solid support. Even at the first meeting the Ascendant player may be aware at some level that Saturn could exert a stabilizing influence on her life, toning down her excesses and offering her a firm anchor. She will frequently view Saturn as a father/mother substitute and often Saturn is indeed older than she, or at least more mature in outlook. If this is the kind of partner the Ascendant player is currently in need of, she too may feel a powerful attraction to Saturn, an attraction which reflects a karmic bondage between the two people, based on a past-life relationship which has been harmonious or inharmonious.

On first acquaintance the two people are unlikely to be aware of any past-life associations, but as they get to know each other better, far-memory recollections of previous shared incarnations may be triggered. Mostly these karmic memories involve some pain and can give rise to apprehensions on the part of both people about committing themselves fully in the present relationship. The subconscious fear of the Ascendant player is that Saturn may re-enact an authoritarian role which frustrated her in an earlier life. Saturn's self-doubt can arise from a subconscious recollection of having previously lost the affection of the Ascendant player due to his inability to express his love for her.

Where the karmic bondage is strong, this preliminary stumbling block is soon overcome and the relationship enters a more secure and settled phase, possibly in the form of a live-in relationship. At this stage the Ascendant player is likely to appreciate the organizational skills of Saturn and his ability to sort out the practical details of living. Above all she will love Saturn for the way he helps her to get things into proportion, calms her when she is upset, reasons with her when she is illogical and generally makes life much easier to cope with. Saturn, too, generally feels fulfilled initially, content to feel needed and valued by the Ascendant player and able to bring about some concrete improvement in her life.

With flowing cross-aspects this harmonious interaction may continue indefinitely, but with hard cross-aspects, where the Ascendant player has negative karma to meet, the honeymoon period can be short-lived and the feelings of Saturn can undergo a gradual and disturbing change. Close daily contact with the Ascendant player makes Saturn increasingly aware of his personality shortcomings and triggers a feeling of inadequacy on his part. Now the satisfaction of knowing he is needed is replaced by the growing belief that he has nothing whatsoever of value to offer his 'perfect' partner.

The defence measures adopted by Saturn to bolster his ego and belittle the Ascendant player consist in withholding all positive feedback in respect of the traits he envies in her, with the result that

80 Relationships, Astrology and Karma

she soon becomes uncomfortable about expressing this side of herself in his presence. Eventually Saturn's coldness may develop into a more generalized, overt criticism of the Ascendant player, focusing especially on her mannerisms, appearance or dress, which can be particularly distressing in a romantic relationship.

The long-term effect of being perpetually ignored can cause the Ascendant player to doubt her own desirability and to fear that Saturn is no longer in love with her, although in reality this may be far from true. Furthermore, the ongoing stress of feeling unable to 'be herself' can seriously affect her physical and mental well-being to the extent that she may decide that the relationship is simply too debilitating and needs to be terminated.

But the outcome is not always so drastic and in many cases the Ascendant player can learn to live with Saturn's tendency to ignore her and failure to give personal compliments. She may learn not to take Saturn's criticism personally, in the knowledge that it arises not from shortcomings on her part but from Saturn's own anxieties and inadequacies. She may come to terms with the dearth of emotional or moral support, coming to rely more on herself and developing a more balanced expression of her Ascendant sign without Saturn's assistance.

But the situation cannot really improve until Saturn acknowledges his envy of the Ascendant player's personality and appearance, stops criticizing and ignoring her and uses her as a role model to develop the qualities he is lacking. It is only when Saturn has reached the stage of acceptance of the Ascendant player and is able to give her positive rather than negative feedback that he can fulfil his true supporting and organizing function. Only then can he provide, in a loving and acceptable form, the stabilizing influence which the Ascendant player needs from him. Only then can he too benefit from the relationship through a willingness both to give and to receive help.

In parent/child relationships, a parent's Saturn in aspect with a child's Ascendant can exert a damaging influence on the child, unless the adult is consciously aware of his resentment towards her and prepared to deal constructively with that resentment. The disapproval to which the child can be subjected from birth by a negative Saturn parent can cause her to grow up with an inferiority complex, self-conscious about 'being herself' and expecting to be found unacceptable by others.

It is especially difficult for a child to cope with the pressure of a relationship with Saturn, since she has no escape route open to her and no way of understanding the psychological motivation of Saturn's attitudes towards her. Although it is possible for an adult to make allowances for Saturnian bad behaviour, it is rare that a child will have the insight or experience to do so, and it is for this reason that we often suffer the full impact of our karma during childhood when we have no means of mitigating the pain.

The cold and overly authoritarian behaviour of such a parent towards his child can be as difficult for the parent as for the child, since it runs counter to a parent's natural desire to express love for his offspring. Yet for a parent whose Saturn is in hard aspect with his child's Ascendant it can be virtually impossible to express warmth spontaneously towards her. Such a parent may fail to understand why the child appears so alien and why she arouses such strong feelings of anger and criticism in him.

It is often immensely difficult for a parent to admit that he has something to learn from his child and that his feelings of hostility are produced by his own inadequacies rather than hers. Yet it is only when a parent comes to this realization and overcomes the persistent desire to nag the child and put her down that a healthy relationship can develop and the negative karmic link can be broken.

An interesting situation arises if it is the child's Saturn which falls on the parent's Ascendant, when the normal roles can appear reversed, with the child chiding the parent and urging him to be more sensible and 'grown up'. Often this is a combination that works well, since the child obtains a good role model and the parent is in the unusually agreeable position of receiving support and commonsense advice from his child. Problems arise only if the parent is prevented from accepting these gifts by his pride or by his need to be seen to be in control.

Cross-aspects involving Saturn have the reputation of being the most 'karmic' of all chart contacts, probably because they can entail long-term service and commitment on the part of one or both of the individuals. They also provide both players with the chance to clear karmic debts by discharging neglected duties, each helping the other to achieve this spiritual cleansing. Mostly it is Saturn who has some past-life obligation to the Ascendant player which he can now fulfil with her co-operation. But not infrequently it is the Ascendant player who has resolved to discharge a karmic responsibility in the area of life ruled by her sign placing and Saturn who has pledged to provide her with the support and encouragement to see this task through.

With Saturn in Libra, Brian had always felt uncomfortable at the one-to-one level. He found it difficult to be spontaneously friendly or make small-talk and through his own self-consciousness he tended to make others feel ill at ease and drive them away.

Perhaps it was because of his own introversion that he found Julie's warmth and openness so attractive. He was instantly spellbound by the dazzling smile characteristic of her Libran Ascendant and her ability to strike up a close relationship so rapidly.

Ironically Julie would never have described herself as good with people. She was aware that she never knew when to say no—partly not to offend people but mainly to avoid losing their friendship— with the result that she spent her life futilely attempting to please others and never pleasing herself. She was certainly a good listener but this only attracted a steady stream of unhappy souls needful of unloading their miseries, who selfishly took advantage of her good nature.

She was in a state of near exhaustion when she met Brian, whose Saturn, almost exactly conjunct her Ascendant, held the promise of the moral support she so badly needed. In many ways it was an attraction of opposites: she was impressed by his ability to keep people at a distance and by his refusal to be pleasant if he didn't wish to be, so unlike herself with her compulsive urge to be 'nice'. When she was in his company she found that this urge diminished and she felt herself to be more confident and more in control. Just a few weeks after their first meeting, her inner sense that Brian was a man she could trust was confirmed by a dream in which, at his bidding, she jumped from a cliff-top and landed safely in his arms.

Six months later they moved in with each other and for the first time in his life Brian had to admit that he was in love. But despite the strength of his feelings for Julie he soon began to experience a curious discontent which he found hard to define. Increasingly he felt overshadowed by her warmth and eloquence which made him acutely aware of his own communication difficulties. When they were in company she always seemed to dominate the conversation with her gushing desire to please, leaving him feeling tongue-tied and left out.

He never discussed his resentments with Julie, mainly because he was hardly conscious of them, but they soon began to express themselves involuntarily when he was alone with her. The enjoyable heart-to-heart discussions which had marked the start of their relationship gradually became a thing of the past as Brian withdrew increasingly into his shell, inhibited by a growing but unrecognized sense of inferiority in relation to Julie.

To Julie, Brian's growing coldness was puzzling and deeply worrying. With her Libran Ascendant, lively conversation was her lifeline and in its absence the whole essence of her being felt deprived and wounded. Although Brian would have been horrified at the suggestion, he had unwittingly found a means of punishing Julie which was very effective indeed.

It was when Julie's health began to break down, giving rise to a variety of allergic symptoms, that she realized she needed to look seriously at her relationship with Brian. She was certainly aware that their communication problem was making her deeply unhappy, but she could not conceive of life without Brian and his practical assistance, support and loyalty. She now relied on him to rationalize her social life by intercepting unwelcome phone-calls and fending off demanding acquaintances. She believed she would be lost without him and feared that he too would be devastated, if she were simply to walk out of the relationship. For despite his coolness he often told her he loved her and needed her, and she knew in her heart that his affection was genuine. Brian, for his part, had no suspicions whatsoever of her unhappiness and was unaware of the impact his taciturnity had upon her.

A transit of Pluto to her Sun gave Julie the impetus to confront the problem head-on, and after some months in therapy she found she could talk over her problems with Brian for the first time. In defence of her charge that he was unresponsive, Brian voiced his disapproval of her insincere over-friendliness and her compulsion to monopolize every conversation. Julie and Brian are currently working towards a compromise: at least they are aware of their dissimilarities and the mutual effect these have on each other.

Saturn–Sun

The admiration Saturn experiences for the Sun on first meeting is less immediate and less physically based than that which he experiences for an Ascendant player, but is nevertheless powerful and likely to lead to a slowly growing interest in the Sun player. Saturn's attention is specifically attracted by the talent represented by the sign occupied by the Sun and the recognition the Sun receives in acknowledgement of that talent. The self-assurance of the Sun and her pride in what she is doing can be deeply intriguing to Saturn, whose own self-esteem is manifestly low in that area. The achievements and confidence of the Sun heighten Saturn's awareness of the kind of person he would like to be and either encourage him to express his hidden creativity or reinforce his sense of inadequacy.

The Sun in turn is likely to feel cautious respect for Saturn, whom she perceives as someone with sufficient organizing ability to help her make more effective use of her abilities. The Sun senses that Saturn, in his maturity, could look after her and take away the burden of life's practicalities, leaving her free to express her creativity with careless abandon. It is unlikely that the Sun will receive much inspiration or open encouragement from Saturn, but what she can expect is a supportive framework within which her talents can blossom.

Subconsciously both the Sun and Saturn can remind each other of key figures from childhood or past lives, the Sun recalling an authority-figure in Saturn, perhaps loved or perhaps hated. Saturn in turn may note the Sun's similarity to an insensitive father-figure responsible for having shattered his self-belief in earlier times.

When these negative associations are present, in order to minimize his sense of inferiority, Saturn may attempt to inhibit the Sun's activities by active interference and discouragement or by subtle criticism, coldness and the withholding of praise. For the Sun, who cannot exist without feedback, such lack of support can be unbearable, can drastically undermine her self-confidence and can destroy her belief in Saturn, whom she had once hoped would have a positive influence on her creativity.

The Sun is more likely to suffer in this way in the case of hard cross-aspects, which suggest the probability of tough karma in her relationship with Saturn and the need for her to take greater personal responsibility for her self-expression without relying on external support.

In the case of flowing cross-aspects, Saturn is less likely to feel threatened by the Sun and more likely to provide her with the practical organization and support she has hoped for. At the same time Saturn will be more open to enjoying and absorbing the vitality and radiance of the Sun, more willing to accept encouragement from her and more able to gain in self-confidence through her example.

But difficulties can arise even when Saturn adopts an encouraging approach, if he projects his unfulfilled ambitions onto the Sun in the hope of experiencing through her the recognition he has been unable to obtain in his own right. Here Saturn may drive the Sun without mercy to make ever greater effort, seemingly never satisfied with her achievements, however high she climbs. This is a common problem when a female Saturn attempts to live out her unexpressed creativity through a male Sun partner; or when a Saturn parent expects his Sun child to manifest the dormant talents fate prevented him from developing. Clearly this places enormous pressure on the Sun partner or Sun child who can push themselves to the limit in a vain effort to win Saturn's approval.

With the conjunction or trine cross-aspect Saturn is more likely to be fundamentally in tune with the Sun's inherent creativity and less likely to have unrealistic expectations of her. But where Saturn is in square or opposition to the Sun, his ambitions for her may bear no relation to her natural abilities, and especially in a parent–child relationship a Saturn parent can direct a Sun child into activities totally inappropriate to her true talents.

With any Saturn cross-aspect, one or both of the two people may feel instinctively that their relationship is a vehicle for the karmic fulfilment of responsibility. In Saturn–Sun cross-aspects Saturn sometimes owes a debt to the Sun which he can discharge by supporting her in her creative self-expression. In other cases it is Saturn's function to help the Sun herself face up to responsibilities in the area of life ruled by her sign position, responsibilities she has neglected persistently in past lives but which must finally be confronted in this incarnation.

In so doing often it is sufficient for Saturn simply to stand back and provide the Sun with unshakeable loyalty, but sometimes he may involuntarily impose unusually heavy responsibilities on his Sun partner, parent or child, thus actively providing them with the opportunity of discharging their karmic debt.

Jane got to know George during a long transit of Saturn over her seventh house cusp, which seemed highly appropriate in that George was 20 years her senior and his Saturn was conjunct her Sun in Aquarius. Jane was just 16 and George was her first serious romance; although she had always made friends easily, she lacked confidence in her sexuality and found it difficult to form close relationships with boys of her own age. But with George she felt completely at ease, capable of being herself in his company without worrying about the impression she was making. He was always so polite and respectful and he made no demands on her, unlike the younger men she had dated who seemed interested in only one thing.

George had been lonely for some time when he met Jane shortly after the break-up of his marriage. He had never been a good mixer and when his wife left him he found himself totally alone with no purpose in his life. He met Jane at work when she joined his firm as a school-leaver, and he was immediately attracted by her outgoing personality. She got on so well with everyone, had a good sense of humour and was always ready to share a laugh with the lads, which he found amazing in one so young.

Despite the disapproval of Jane's parents, she married George, bore his child and for a couple of years felt blissfully secure and protected in the warmth of his gentle love. George, for his part, had found a brand new direction in life in the form of his young family and for the first time ever he felt totally needed and fulfilled.

Problems arose only when Jane returned to work at George's firm and began to rebuild her social life which had been non-existent since her marriage. To her surprise, she found that not only did George discourage her from making new friends, but he actually tried to obstruct her. She enjoyed going out with a crowd from work, perhaps for a lunchtime drink, perhaps for an evening meal, but George always refused to join in and showed his resentment by sulking if she went without him. She tried to get round the problem by bringing girlfriends back to their home, but George's blatant rudeness made her unwilling to invite them again.

The fact was that George was deeply jealous of his young wife's popularity and afraid it would only be a matter of time before she found someone younger and more fun than himself. He knew himself to be staid and inept in group situations and tried to avoid exposing his inadequacy by shunning all social gatherings. He relied totally on Jane for adult company, having no friends of his own and never going out except to work, and he now attempted to make her equally dependent on him in the hope this would prevent her from straying.

In effect the reverse came about in that George's attempts to restrict Jane drove her away from him rather than bringing her closer. Certainly she had no intention of leaving him since she valued the love and stability she received from him. But at the same time she knew that unless she made a life of her own she could easily become bitter and end up hating him, which was something she didn't want to happen.

Nowadays Jane has many friends and indulges in the occasional semi-serious affair, although these have never threatened her marriage to George. She has learned to put up with his criticism and disapproval and overall is content with her lot in life. George has turned a blind eye to his young partner's infidelities and he too is thankful for the companionship and affection he enjoys from her. Against all the odds they have managed to come to terms with their differences and are making a success of a relationship many thought unviable.

Saturn–Moon

When the Moon first encounters Saturn she can experience a tremendous relief at having at last found a source of emotional support and a shoulder to cry on. Often Saturn will be older than she, or at least more emotionally mature and is frequently perceived by the Moon as an older brother or older sister substitute.

When Saturn's emotional disposition is indeed as mature as the Moon would like to believe it to be, Saturn will be ready to listen to and empathize with her feelings whilst offering advice of a commonsense nature. He will be capable of calming and balancing the emotional excesses of the Moon, always pointing out the practical considerations and helping her to get her anxieties into perspective.

Saturn can often discharge an obligation to the Moon incurred in a past-life encounter by providing her now with support at the feeling level; alternatively he may enable the Moon to clear a karmic debt by encouraging her to fulfil hitherto neglected emotional or nurturing responsibilities.

But when Saturn is not in touch with his spiritual purpose or has not yet come to terms with his own emotional problems, he may disappoint the Moon's hopes of emotional support, offering criticism instead of sympathy and pessimism instead of encouragement. This is most often the case when social inhibitions repress Saturn's instinctive mode of self-expression—a mode of self-expression with which he is confronted in the feelings, moods or mannerisms of the Moon. Here Saturn will treat the Moon with the same austerity as he treats himself, chastising her for her foolishness, her weakness, or her socially unacceptable behaviour.

Saturn's neurotic desire to subdue the Moon can have its roots in her resemblance to a mother-figure from his past, a mother-figure who sowed the seeds of his present sense of inadequacy and from whom he now seeks to protect himself. For Saturn the best means of self-defence is to withdraw behind a hard and impenetrable wall, which habitually confronts the Moon when she approaches Saturn for comfort and sympathy.

When the Moon is closely in touch with her karmic destiny, she may sense instinctively that Saturn's presence in her life is intended to toughen her up a little. She may succeed in ignoring his harshness and unkindness and in taking responsibility for her own emotions without constant need of his reassurance. But often the persistent lack of empathy can give rise to deep loneliness and perhaps depression on her part, and she may eventually feel compelled to break free from the emotional prison to which she is consigned by Saturn.

Behind Saturn's defensiveness lies a profound irritability, a simmering, well-controlled anger towards the Moon for her uninhibited and carefree expression of the very feelings he works so hard to control and expends so much energy in repressing. With his characteristic self-discipline, the nearest Saturn can come to giving voice to his irritability is to nag the Moon, often mercilessly and with unflinching continuity.

Nagging is perhaps the most typical feature of a hard Saturn–Moon cross-aspect, which can insidiously poison any relationship over a period of years. In many a Saturn–Moon marriage the two partners can feel obliged to stick things out for the sake of duty and propriety, whilst harbouring a mutual grudge which guarantees a further karmic encounter.

The nagging of a Saturn parent can rob a Moon child of much of her spontaneous emotional self-expression as she learns to keep her feelings to herself rather than risk rebuke or ridicule from a seemingly uncaring mother or father—a pattern which frequently results in psychological difficulties for the child later in life.

Here, and especially in a mother–child relationship, normal parental tenderness can be absent in the Saturn player, who may well love the child sincerely but feel too awkward or inadequate to show love for her. A similar problem can exist for a mother when her child's Saturn is in aspect with her own Moon, in that the child simply refuses to respond to the mother's affection however hard she tries to express it.

Mike had come through a tough upbringing with more than a few emotional scars to show for it. The last and somewhat puny child to be born in a family of three girls, he had failed to receive the usual petting and spoiling from his sisters, who nagged and bullied him when he was too small to fight back. One sister in particular took every opportunity to prove her power over Mike, a favourite trick of hers being to bang his head against a wall until, helpless to retaliate, he gave in to her humiliating demands.

Saturn in Aries in Mike's chart symbolized the frustrated rage he had carried with him since early childhood. He often felt violently angry in response to some personal insult or injustice but was unable to give external expression to his anger, which manifested internally instead in the form of a chronic stomach ulcer.

He initially felt disappointed that the only child of his marriage was a girl, since he had hoped that a son might embody the assertiveness he feared he was lacking and thus fortify his low self-esteem. Maybe it was because of this projection that Clare, his daughter, showed early signs of an independent and forceful temperament. She was quick to speak her mind and enjoyed confrontations in a way that was unusual for little girls of her generation; seemingly she was just the kind of child that Mike had longed for to live out his own repressed aggression.

But perhaps because such behaviour was unacceptable to him in a girl, or perhaps because his Saturn fell in close conjunction with Clare's Moon in Aries, Mike's reaction to his daughter's angry outbursts was to feel disturbed and deeply threatened. The fact was that Clare's assertiveness stirred up his deep-seated sense of inadequacy and left him at a loss as to how to handle her. And although he was never consciously aware of the fact, Clare's close resemblance to his elder sister invoked a deep dislike in him for his daughter, a dislike which was kindled into smouldering fury by what he perceived as her insolence towards him.

And so it was that throughout her childhood Clare's naturally ebullient disposition met with the acrimonious disapproval of her father. At first she experienced this disapproval simply through his cold withdrawal from her and his cutting comments that with her temper she didn't fit into the family.

But as Clare grew older, her growing rebelliousness and argumentativeness characteristic of all teenagers triggered an almost neurotic antipathy in Mike, which he expressed in manic outpourings of ugly verbal abuse towards her. He found it increasingly difficult to control a desire to strike, even to murder, his daughter when she 'spoke out of turn', although physical violence was against all his ethics.

By the time Clare was 14 Mike was subjecting her to regular emotional abuse, which included threats to kill her if she challenged his authority. With his greater strength, Mike gradually succeeded in undermining his daughter's assertiveness, as she realized the only way to win his approval was to keep her feelings to herself and smile calmly, whatever rage she was experiencing inside.

Clearly it was a re-enactment of Mike's own childhood karma. Like her father before her, Clare learned to hold in her emotions and refrain from asserting herself for fear of the consequences, although such acquiescent behaviour ran counter to her true instincts. As a young adult she struggled for many years with an inability to acknowledge her own anger or to handle others' anger towards her, which naturally had an adverse effect on her relationships. Of course she still felt angry with people, but she expressed her fury by cutting herself off from them, never by exposing her passionate feelings.

Clare's hatred towards her father for his cruelty to her ceased only on his death, at which she felt a guilty relief. By then she was married, and with the help of a patient and understanding husband gradually rebuilt her trust in her spontaneous emotions and the self-confidence to express these, however challenging to others, without the fear of losing their affection or suffering abuse.

Saturn–Mercury

It is a sober type of attraction that exists between Saturn and Mercury, but it is an attraction none the less and harmonious cross-aspects between these two planets can frequently result in lasting friendships based on a meeting of minds. In the case of a positive combination, Mercury can find a patient and willing listener in Saturn, particularly appreciated by Mercury when she herself finds verbal self-expression difficult and has had problems in the past in finding a sympathetic ear. Also, for the first time, Mercury may discover in Saturn someone who is prepared to take her seriously, give credence to her ideas and offer constructive or practical advice. This too can prove comforting to a Mercury who has been accustomed to having her ideas dismissed or ridiculed.

For Saturn, the attraction of Mercury usually resides in her voice, the tone and rhythm of her speech, and her body language, all of which reflect her mental energy, an energy to which Saturn is especially drawn since he is aware of its absence in his own psyche. The attraction experienced by Saturn also encompasses the desire to assist and give support to Mercury, often by providing instruction in an area of life in which he has more knowledge and practical experience than she.

Frequently Saturn's attraction is based on the subconscious awareness that he has a karmic debt to repay to Mercury, or that his function in this lifetime is to help Mercury to discharge a previously unfulfilled responsibility relating to her verbal or intellectual self-expression.

Saturn actually represents the perfect teacher for Mercury since he has clear insight into any weaknesses in her reasoning, judgement and her ability to communicate effectively. The help Saturn has to offer may not be inspirational, but it can serve to organize and structure Mercury's thinking or to stimulate serious and logical discussion. Indeed Mercury is often encouraged by Saturn to develop her intellectual gifts or to take up a practical form of study. Sometimes the two people will decide to enter into a business relationship with each other, in which it is Mercury who supplies the ideas and Saturn the pragmatic back-up.

Saturn–Mercury is a combination which lends itself best to working or learning relationships but can often seem out of place in a romantic partnership, where Mercury may resent Saturn's attempts to improve her mind and to prove he is the cleverer of the two. Difficulties occur mainly when Saturn feels inadequate in the sphere of life symbolized by the sign placing of his partner's Mercury and feels threatened when Mercury gives voice to that side of himself he is most self-conscious about expressing. In the case of a square aspect between Saturn and Mercury, the mere note and tone of Mercury's voice is sufficient to make Saturn sadly aware of the quality lacking in himself and to cause him to adopt tough defence tactics in order to preserve his ego.

When Saturn goes on the defensive, he will attempt to gag Mercury to prevent her from discussing subject areas with which he feels uneasy or from talking in a way that causes him embarrassment. It is never easy to make Mercury hold her tongue, but Saturn has some cunning tricks up his sleeve, like the art of constantly picking holes in her reasoning, semantics or use of grammar. Saturn's petty quibbling over use of language may eventually wear down the Mercury partner, who may come to feel she can never get through to Saturn and may eventually completely give up trying.

In the case of inharmonious cross-aspects Mercury may perceive Saturn as a very poor listener and may complain bitterly that she cannot make herself heard by Saturn, who is actually much too afraid to listen to Mercury or to accept what she has to say. In some cases Mercury may find no mental rapport whatsoever with Saturn and may be thrown back on her own intellectual resources, for which she must now take karmic responsibility.

Saturn's tendency to find fault with Mercury's intellect or speech is especially damaging when Mercury is lacking in confidence in these areas, and even more so when Mercury is a child. Here the Saturn parent's over-concern with and criticism of young Mercury's academic progress can undermine the child's belief in her mental abilities or cause her to abandon her schooling prematurely. In other cases she can be driven to push herself beyond her mental and physical resources in her studies and to worry obsessively about examination results, often with tragic consequences.

The situation may be even more fraught when it is the child who plays Saturn to his mother or father's Mercury, since few parents are prepared to accept criticism of their arguments or their speech from a 'know-it-all' youngster who constantly interrupts them, even in company. But however infuriating it is for a parent to be corrected by their offspring, the Mercury adult may well have something to learn from her Saturn child in terms of communication skills. Frequently the parent–child roles of the two players were reversed in their last incarnation together, where the current child was an instructor or authority-figure and the current parent was a pupil or dependent. A parent with sufficient humility will often be willing to acknowledge her Saturn child's greater wisdom.

Linda had always had an interest in astrology, so when she discovered that her Saturn in Leo was exactly square to her baby son's Mercury in Scorpio she had some anxious moments as to how their relationship would unfold. But she believed that to be forewarned was to be forearmed and firmly resolved to avoid falling into the negative Saturn role. Little did she realize just how difficult this would prove.

John, her son, had been born with a tongue-tie which the doctors had assured her was in need of no treatment. But it soon became apparent that John had greater than average difficulty in articulating words, a problem which troubled Linda considerably though she never spoke of her concern to anyone. In fact it was John's slowness in learning to talk that initiated Linda's obsessive preoccupation with his speech, a preoccupation of which she was certainly aware but which she could seemingly do nothing about, despite her astrological insights.

The main problem was that John's slight speech impediment made it difficult for his mother to understand him, which obliged her to ask him continuously to repeat himself. One side of her knew she should play down John's speech problem to prevent him from feeling self-conscious. But another side insisted on drawing attention to his disability as a means of hitting back at him when he made her angry—which was something that happened with increasing frequency as he grew older and more rebellious.

It was John's forceful way of talking to her as a teenager and his irritating ability to win every argument, which triggered Linda's distinctly unmotherly urge to put him down by whatever means she could. Unable to defeat him by logical discussion, she fell back on her old habit of criticizing his speech, although by now his speech impediment had virtually disappeared. She felt justified in using this means of attack, since she resented what she viewed as John's bullying and saw no other means of preventing him from getting the better of her.

Because she had always seen John as the stronger person and had failed to appreciate the undermining influence her criticism had exerted on him over the years, she was surprised and hurt when he began to accuse her of doubting his intelligence and treating him as a half-wit. His progress at school had been unspectacular compared to that of his academically gifted elder brother, who had received all the praise from Linda, and this added fuel to his sense of intellectual inferiority and to his conviction that his mother had no faith in him.

To give Linda her due, she had tried to encourage John in his school work and to coach him in the subjects she had some proficiency in, but he had always rejected her offers of help, complaining that she expected too much of him and made the work too boring. It was at this point that she became aware of the huge gulf that had developed between them and she recalled with dismay the Mercury–Saturn square which had apparently all but destroyed her relationship with John.

She knew it would be difficult to undo the damage that had been done, but she resolved to set about forging a friendship with her child before it was finally too late. A Pluto transit to her Sun allowed her to face and let go of her fear of the power of John's will, helped her to learn to talk to him as an equal and to overcome her expectation that he would always beat her down and injure her pride. She also began to look for a means of expressing her creativity now that the children were almost off her hands and joined the local amateur dramatic society, despite her apprehensiveness.

As Linda learned to claim her own power she found that her relationship with John became increasingly less threatening and by the time John had reached his late teens she found she really enjoyed chatting to him on all manner of subjects. She now came to appreciate the outspokenness she had once dreaded and to value the time and energy he devoted to exploring some point of philosophy with her. But perhaps her greatest joy came from John's acknowledgement that she was a good listener, a compliment she was uncertain she deserved but which she fully intended to earn in the future.

Saturn–Venus

When Venus is somewhat lacking in confidence in her appearance, her sex appeal or her ability to make friends, a harmonious relationship with Saturn can provide the emotional security to help boost her self-assurance. A good Saturn will provide Venus with moral support without making demands on her or having any expectations of her. She can relax in his company in the knowledge that he will not judge her and will accept her as she is with all her social or physical imperfections. In a supportive relationship of this kind Saturn will invariably have greater maturity than Venus, either in years or in attitude.

Even when Venus is of a more confident disposition, she can still receive practical help from Saturn, who will take a serious interest in her leisure pursuits, promote her artistic activities and organize her finances, particularly useful when Venus is scatter-brained by nature.

It is true that even with the most harmonious of cross-aspects Venus is unlikely to find much sparkle in her relationship with Saturn. But what she will gain is a sense of commitment on his part and a feeling of emotional safety within the relationship. Venus frequently senses at a subconscious level that she has been drawn towards Saturn because he has a karmic responsibility towards her which he must discharge in this lifetime. Or she may realize that the purpose of her meeting with Saturn is to help her face up to her own karmic responsibilities within relationships.

Saturn's initial response to Venus can be uncomfortable yet compulsive. He usually experiences an uneasy admiration of her looks, clothes and style, which reflect qualities he believes are absent in himself but which he would dearly love to possess. Saturn's envy of Venus can derive not merely from her appearance but also from her social skills, her creative talent or even her financial assets, all of which can arouse a sense of inadequacy in Saturn if he feels himself to be wanting in any of these areas.

With a harmonious cross-aspect, or when Saturn is capable of coming to terms with and containing his feelings of inadequacy and envy, he will be able to enjoy the beauty and charm Venus can introduce into his life and to feel 'complete', perhaps for the first time, when in her company. In turn he will be ready and willing to help Venus to maximize her talents and assets.

But when Venus has challenging karma to face in her relationship with Saturn, he may be less able to handle his negative feelings towards her and more likely to indulge in open or disguised criticism of her style, her tastes or her handling of resources. When Saturn reacts in this way, his antagonism towards Venus may be intensified by her resemblance to a female sibling or peer whom he knew earlier in the present life or in a past life and who caused him to feel aesthetically inadequate.

In a sexual relationship a negative Saturn can slowly undermine Venus's confidence in her desirability by persistently failing to compliment her or by drawing attention to her flaws. And the harder Venus tries to recapture the flagging interest of her ungracious partner, often by extravagant spending on clothes and beauty treatments, the more disapproving Saturn becomes of her wastefulness and the more hardened to her charms.

This, plus the total absence on Saturn's part of those little romantic gestures that make Venus feel wanted, can reinforce any existing self-doubt in Venus and can eventually dent the pride of even the most self-assured Venus of either sex. Venus's confidence in dealing with people, handling money or expressing herself artistically can also be worn down by the cool or downright critical response of Saturn. And in the absence of Saturn's constructive advice she may have to learn to take responsibility for her own aesthetic and social values.

Saturnian jealousy can spring up in any type of one-to-one contact and even parent–child relationships are not immune to this problem. Especially among parents and children of the same sex, the sense of inadequacy experienced by a Saturn parent confronted with a good-looking Venus son or daughter can inhibit the Saturn parent's capacity for a warm and supportive relationship with the child. In some cases the parent may unwittingly place obstacles in the path of the child which prevent it from fulfilling its true creative potential. In others the parent may subject the child to excessive pressure to achieve, in the hope that the child will live out his own unfulfilled artistic ambitions.

As the middle child of three sisters, Anna had missed out on her fair share of nurturing. Since early childhood she had been violently jealous of her younger sister both for 'stealing' her parents' affection and because of her striking good looks, which she saw as the reason why she attracted so much attention.

It may have been on this account that Anna's adult relationships with women were marred by envy and mistrust, and that when she became pregnant her preference was for a boy. The birth of her daughter Jill was a disappointment she tried hard to conceal, but a conjunction between her Saturn in the early degrees of Cancer and the child's Venus at the end of Gemini spelled out the cold and difficult mother–daughter relationship that was destined to ensue.

At first things ran smoothly but as Jill approached puberty, her mother's disinterest in all aspects of her femininity set up an emotional gulf which denied them the usual mother–daughter closeness. Anna's strong disapproval of make-up and fashionable clothes cast a shadow over Jill's adolescent discovery of her sexuality and caused her to feel uncomfortable and self-conscious about looking attractive.

It was not that Anna didn't love her daughter, for in many ways she was a model mother, forsaking a career to ensure her child lacked no home comforts. Indeed, what Jill appreciated most about her mother was that she was always there, always able to provide the hot meals and clean clothes that represent the material security of childhood. What was lacking, however, was any kind of emotional rapport and as Jill grew older she envied the easy-going relationship many of her girlfriends enjoyed with their mothers, who seemed able to discuss all manner of adolescent problems without any of the embarrassment she experienced with Anna.

From the start Anna's problem had been that, for some reason she didn't understand, she felt physically incapable of demonstrating her love for her daughter. Spontaneous displays of affection didn't come easily to her and she rarely kissed Jill even at bedtime. She found it impossible to utter the usual terms of maternal endearment: words such as 'darling' or 'pet' stuck in her throat and seemed strangely inappropriate. Although she knew herself to be a responsible and dutiful mother, Anna was aware that something held her back from giving fully of herself to Jill, but just what this was she never attempted to discover.

The root of Anna's coldness was actually her transference onto Jill of her long-standing jealousy towards her younger sister, manifest in her tendency to call Jill mistakenly by her sister's name. Ever since Jill's birth she had feared the child might take her place in her husband's affections, just as her sister had robbed her of her parents' love so many years before. And as she witnessed the fading of her own looks just when Jill's were beginning to blossom, this fear grew ever stronger.

The fact was that Anna was unconsciously jealous of her daughter and not simply of her youthful good looks but also of her intelligence and her career prospects in journalism. She felt that Jill's ambitions highlighted her own inadequacies and failures, and outsiders' comments that her daughter in no way resembled her only fuelled her fear that she would be compared unfavourably with Jill, especially by her husband.

Jill may well have tolerated her mother's coldness indefinitely, but it was when she began to interfere in her choice of boyfriends that matters were brought finally to an angry head. The strict rules of conduct which Anna laid down, her constant moral interrogations and her obvious lack of trust in her daughter were anathema to Jill's natal Venus/Uranus conjunction and an affront to her personal integrity. She knew she would never feel free to express her sexuality joyfully in her mother's austere presence. So under the influence of transiting Uranus square natal Uranus she left home for good at the age of 18, since when her contact with her mother has been sporadic and cool.

Saturn–Mars

With every Saturn cross-aspect the initial response of both individuals can be one of subtle and ill-defined fascination. When Mars is involved the fascination is sexually orientated and thus more readily identifiable, although invariably still relatively slow to unfold.

With her predatory approach, Mars is initially challenged by the incongruity of Saturn's attraction to her yet his seeming aloofness to her advances. Frequently she will experience a powerful urge to prove her sexual prowess by arousing the cool and well controlled Saturn; Mars's chief interest lies in the possibility of conquest and the tougher the conquest the greater the glory.

Despite his failure to demonstrate his feelings, Saturn can indeed be mesmerized by Mars, especially by her open demonstration of her passion and sexuality in a way that he himself finds embarrassing and difficult. It is Mars's spontaneous and fearless expression of the qualities which Saturn most admires but feels he is lacking which spellbinds him to Mars and causes him to feel a whole person in her company. There is something of the voyeur in Saturn in his desire to observe and feed off Mars's passion as a compensation for the void in his own life.

As with all Saturn cross-aspects, there is usually some debt of responsibility to be paid, often on the part of Saturn who may be subconsciously aware of an obligation to provide Mars with practical support, sometimes in her work or career or simply by helping her to channel her energy more effectively. In a harmonious karmic relationship, Saturn can act as a useful stopcock on Mars's adrenalin flow, helping her to check excessive emotional outpourings and to utilize that energy for concrete goals. In this way Saturn can encourage Mars to discharge her own karmic responsibilities by fulfilling tasks which require energetic commitment and which have been neglected by her in past lives.

The notorious problems long attributed to Saturn–Mars cross-aspects occur only when Mars is destined to meet with hard karma at the hands of Saturn, in which case Saturn can certainly make life very frustrating for her and may oblige her to pay back her karmic debt under harsh conditions.

When Saturn is unkind to Mars, his behaviour may be triggered by his association of Mars with a male peer or sibling whose greater strength or assertiveness humiliated him in the past and contributed towards his current sense of inadequacy in the sphere of life symbolized by Mars's placing. When this transference occurs, Saturn can feel driven to punish Mars for his past pain and to assume a position of control in which he feels less vulnerable. It is essentially by quenching Mars's passions that Saturn is best able to achieve this control and it is especially in the area of sexual relationships that this strategy can produce the greatest problems.

A Saturn–Mars sexual relationship can be surprisingly good at first due to Mars's provocative attentions to Saturn and Saturn's initial infatuation. But Saturn's increasing need to prove his mastery of Mars can later manifest as ever more frequent rejections of his partner's sexual advances, which can gradually dampen the libido of even the most passionate Mars.

It is not only in terms of sex that Mars can feel emasculated by Saturn, but also in any expression of her deepest feelings, such as anger, fear or grief. Saturn's tactics are often based on a refusal to be drawn into any form of confrontation, which deprives Mars of an outlet for her passions and forces them back into her psyche. The result is that Mars finds it increasingly difficult to give effective vent to her feelings when in the company of Saturn and can feel profoundly rejected by Saturn at the level of her very life-force.

A Saturn–Mars contact often produces a master–slave relationship when Saturn's urge to obtain maximum efficiency from Mars leads him to drive her excessively in her career or domestic responsibilities—perhaps through the best of intentions or perhaps with the unconscious desire to put Mars in her place. This can be a particular problem for Mars when she connives with Saturn by pushing herself beyond her limits as a demonstration of her endurance, which she hopes will recapture Saturn's respect.

Saturn often adopts a slave-driving role when he is the parent of a Mars child, exploiting the child's instinctive desire to please and to earn approval through her successes. By instilling Mars with the belief that her victories are never quite good enough, Saturn can distort the child's future attitude to achievement, creating a workaholic or loser complex. Saturn can also adversely influence his Martian child's psychological development by inhibiting her ability to express passionate feelings spontaneously and by punishing the child for overt expression of anger, tears or sexuality.

For a child with a negative Saturn parent, and for a man or woman with a negative Saturn partner, the karmic challenge can consist in learning to assert oneself without support in the area of life symbolized by the sign placing of Mars, in being prepared to acknowledge and express one's deepest passions even in the face of disapproval, and in being willing to claim one's power as an individual even when others attempt to strip it from us.

Before they got together neither Angie nor Don had achieved very much in their lives. Both were in jobs they disliked but which they continued with simply for the income. Both were into drink, Don in quite a big way. Neither was using their creative talents and neither had been involved in a loving long-term relationship. But all this was to change soon after they moved in with each other, at which time their lifestyle changed abruptly from one of aimlessness to one of workaholic intensity.

A two-way Saturn–Mars contact between their charts symbolized the strong initial sexual pull which nevertheless proved difficult to consummate. From the start they had mutual difficulty in interpreting each other's body language, and on their first date each was convinced that the other found them sexually unattractive simply because neither gave the appropriate signals.

But somehow the relationship survived this ineptness and when they did finally sleep together they were genuinely surprised at just how good their sex-life turned out to be. After years of frigidity Angie had her first real orgasm and with Don she found the ability to be sexually adventurous in a way she had never thought possible. As for Don, his relationship with Angie was the first which combined lust with friendship, giving the sexual act a new depth and meaning for him.

They also had a mutually beneficial influence on each other's working life in that both gave up drinking and began to make more productive use of their leisure hours. Angie took up writing, something she had wanted to do for many years but had convinced herself she had no time for, whilst Don began a course of study which he hoped would allow him to embark on a new career as a teacher.

It was after about one year that the early sexual inhibitions began to creep back insidiously into the relationship and the original problem of body language signals re-emerged. Don felt increasingly that Angie didn't respond to his foreplay, which turned him off and caused him to lose interest. Angie resented the fact that as soon as she became aroused Don's passion appeared to cool, leaving her bewildered and frustrated. As the go-stop pattern of their sexual interaction established itself, each became increasingly distrustful of the other and their love-making became less and less frequent. The sexual dissatisfaction experienced by both of them expressed itself as emotional withdrawal on the part of Don and nagging ill temper on the part of Angie.

A contributory factor towards their failed love-life was their constant state of physical exhaustion, induced by the strict working routine which had initially given them a new sense of purpose, but which now dominated their lives and sapped their libido. As time passed, each found it increasingly difficult to relax in the other's company and each felt guilty if they weren't working when the other was busy. Don, who had always sensed that Angie was critical of his previous underachievement, now felt under constant pressure from her to succeed with his studies and obtain a prestigious post, which had the effect of reinforcing his fear of failure and the possibility of Angie's rejection.

Angie in turn felt she needed to be some kind of superwoman in order to win Don's approval: he had always said he could not respect a woman without a career in her own right, but he also expected her to shoulder most of the domestic jobs and keep the household running like clockwork. Each was of the opinion that idleness was a sin in the eyes of the other, with the effect that by bedtime neither had any energy left for love-making or for any other form of emotional sharing.

Eventually each came to believe, unbeknown to the other, that their love affair was dead and parting inevitable. Don wanted a fuller sexual relationship than that offered by Angie and was fast reaching the point of seeking a new lover. For Angie, it was not so much sex that she felt was missing in the relationship as tenderness and emotional closeness, without which she felt she had no evidence of Don's love.

Fortunately their deep karmic connection enabled them to attempt to sort out their difficulties before it was finally too late. Realizing that spontaneity was not their strong point, they planned set times in the day just to be with each other and satisfy each other's sexual and emotional needs. This timetable love-making proved the perfect solution for Don and Angie, because each knew what was expected of them, and when, and there was no chance of disappointing each other. Basically it was a question of their allowing one another time off, something which is always difficult in a Saturn–Mars interaction, which does not lend itself easily to leisure or to frivolousness.

THE KARMIC
CROSS-ASPECTS OF URANUS

Uranus–Ascendant

Cross-aspects involving Uranus are the most magnetic, compelling and tantalizing of all interpersonal contacts. They symbolize relationships based on love at first sight, mind-blowing infatuations which flare up and die down unpredictably, relationships in which two people cannot live without each other but may often find it difficult to live *with* each other. They may not guarantee permanence, but what they do offer is an adventure in mutual self-discovery, an opportunity for two people to explore their individuality with each other's encouragement.

When Uranus in one chart is in aspect with the Ascendant of another, the sense of mutual exhilaration is particularly marked and more likely to withstand the effects of familiarity and time than most other Uranus cross-aspects. Romantic relationships based on this cross-aspect have the ability to keep the flame of passion alive indefinitely, albeit with intermittent cooling of feelings or occasional partings.

For Uranus, contact with the Ascendant player has a powerfully liberating influence. Through the physical presence of the Ascendant player Uranus is motivated and encouraged to cast off his inhibitions, spurn convention and be more true to himself and his idiosyncrasies. Even the most strait-laced of individuals becomes more of a free spirit when in the company of someone whose Ascendant degree resonates with their Uranus, the planetary symbol of their urge for independence.

The Ascendant player at the receiving end of Uranus's uninhibited behaviour cannot but be ensnared, for there is nothing as appealing as someone who is being utterly himself, unselfconsciously and without any barriers. Excitement is the main emotion experienced by the Ascendant player, a thrilling expectation of that which is different and unpredictable. For the Ascendant player Uranus holds the promise of someone who may bring important change into her life, who may hold the key to releasing her from a boring emotional, mental or physical rut.

The anticipation of the Ascendant player is not always joyful, however. When the Ascendant player has fixed behaviour patterns, her desire for the new may be tinged with dread of losing the old. And when the relationship is a re-enactment of an unhappy past-life contact, she may experience far memories of disruption and chaos which she fears may recur in this incarnation. Early on in a love affair the Ascendant player must decide whether she can accommodate the insecurity and unpredictability which she senses will form an integral part of the relationship. There can be no such thing as a steady relationship with Uranus, however much the Ascendant player believes this may be possible.

The subconscious reactions of Uranus may likewise be based on a past-life relationship with the Ascendant player, a relationship which has inspired Uranus to render karmic service to her in this lifetime by helping her achieve a higher level of independence and freedom. There is often the realization on the part of Uranus that he can be instrumental in broadening the horizons of the Ascendant player; and if he has sufficient humility he may also be aware that he too can receive stimulating insights through the qualities and talents of the Ascendant player.

The speed at which Uranus–Ascendant relationships develop can be phenomenal. In a sexual relationship it is not uncommon for the two people to sleep with each other on the first date and to move in with each other or get married after only two weeks. For this reason such relationships may also come to a premature and unexpectedly sudden end, but whatever their duration they invariably compress into a comparatively short period of time a range and depth of experience which many couples spend a lifetime acquiring.

Even with the most mutually beneficial of contacts, Uranus relationships always follow a spasmodic pattern of highs and lows, of togetherness and distance. Frequently they are part-time relationships in which the two people live apart or see each other only at weekends, as in extramarital affairs. Or in a standard live-in relationship they may see relatively little of each other due to working or leisure commitments. In every case discontinuity forms an integral part of the relationship, for it is only by this means that stagnation can be avoided and the novelty so necessary for ongoing stimulation can be maintained. It seems that infrequency of contact is the key whereby the two people can keep alive their fascination for each other and constantly introduce new challenges into each other's lives.

When a Uranus–Ascendant cross-aspect is operating harmoniously inasmuch as the level of the interaction is mutually fulfilling, this intermittent contact can be refreshing to both individuals. Uranus can provide the Ascendant player with opportunities to expand her understanding and experience in the area of life ruled by the Ascendant sign; in turn the Ascendant player can supply Uranus with ongoing inspiration to devise ever newer and more thrilling adventures for their mutual diversion.

The success of the relationship is dependent upon Uranus's ability to keep within reasonable bounds his inherent distaste for restriction. When Uranus's longing for freedom takes precedence over his love and commitment to the Ascendant player, the unstable, disruptive aspect of the relationship becomes exaggerated and is experienced as disturbing by the Ascendant player—unless she too has Uranian characteristics. When this happens the Ascendant player is invariably meeting with her own past-life misuse of freedom through her present-life relationship with wayward Uranus.

When Uranus goes off the rails, it is a reflection of his fear that his deepening affection for the Ascendant player poses a threat to his continued independence and an attempt to gain some detachment before he is well and truly hooked. Sometimes this fear is accentuated by the Ascendant player's resemblance to a figure from his past by whom he was once imprisoned emotionally, mentally or physically and from whom he now must protect himself. In other cases his resistance to commitment is motivated simply by his apprehension of the vast change in emotional or mental outlook that a close, ongoing relationship would involve. The greater this fear becomes on his part, the worse his behaviour towards the Ascendant player and the greater the risk to the viability of the relationship.

Uranus's attempts to wriggle free can manifest as an unpredictable tendency to break arrangements with the Ascendant player, to reject her desire for emotional closeness, or to argue excessively about ideas which she cannot accept or understand. The Ascendant player may find that her instinctive self-expression and her basic relationship needs—as symbolized by her Ascendant –Descendant axis—are periodically held up to ridicule by Uranus. Small wonder that in many love affairs the Ascendant player soon comes to believe that Uranus's ardour is cooling and that she should extricate herself without delay before she really gets hurt.

Uranus's unreliability is easier to tolerate in a platonic friendship than in a sexual relationship, where anything less than total loyalty and commitment can be interpreted as faithlessness, or in a parent–child relationship where the parent's ongoing presence is important to the child's healthy development. However, when an Ascendant child has challenging karma to face through the instrument of a Uranian parent, stability is invariably lacking in her early life, especially in terms of the sign ruling the Ascendant. There is little that a child can do in such circumstances other than develop sufficient independence and adaptability to cope with her Uranian parent's unpredictability. But in a sexual relationship an insecure Ascendant partner will often attempt to cling to Uranus or tie him down, sometimes by appealing to his better nature, sometimes by crass emotional blackmail.

But whatever her tactics, the fact is that there is no means whereby the Ascendant player can coerce Uranus into greater closeness, for Uranus has no emotional need of the Ascendant player and no compunction to remain in the relationship if it is no longer fun. In the eyes of Uranus, a possessive, whining and obstructive Ascendant partner is anything but fun and will usually be abandoned for a less demanding lover.

The Ascendant player who is neglected by a Uranian partner ultimately has little choice other than to build a life of her own, either within the framework of the relationship or after a separation from Uranus. If her karmic bondage to Uranus is to be broken, it is important for her to accept the freedom granted to her with gratitude rather than bitterness and to understand the karmic purpose of the relationship.

Karen was fresh out of convent school when she met Jay, whose

Uranus fell exactly on her Cancer Ascendant. Although approximately the same age as herself, he was a good deal more mature, having been left to his own devices after his mother walked out on the family when he was just 12. In contrast to her own strict middle-class upbringing, he had enjoyed almost total freedom as a teenager and had his first sexual relationship with a girl when only 14. Jay was streetwise, totally independent and unlike any boy Karen had previously encountered. He had so many fascinating tales to recount about his back-packing abroad, about the commune he had lived in for a couple of months, and about the bohemian world he now inhabited, which aroused a longing in Karen to become part of that world and to give her love to this wild, uncivilized gypsy of a boy.

His trust in women having been shattered by his mother's desertion, Jay had always tended to keep his girlfriends at a distance. Because he had learned to cook, to do his own laundry and provide for himself at an early age, he had always believed he had no need of a live-in girlfriend and had seen girls mainly as sexual playmates.

True to form, he was sleeping with Karen after only their second date, not unusual for him but entirely out of character for Karen who was still a virgin and had always believed she would remain so until after she was married. She knew from the start that she was crazy about Jay, whereas for him it might well have been just another affair until he realized, to his amazement, that she was becoming indispensable to him.

She was the first girl in his life who had cooked for him, or whom he had given permission to cook for him. She was the first girl who worried about whether he had clean underwear or clean bed linen, and despite his fierce self-reliance he found he quite enjoyed the attention. The fact was that Karen's mothering actually increased his freedom, releasing him from household chores for more mind-expanding activities. The arrangement suited him perfectly—a live-out lover who satisfied his sexual and domestic needs but made no emotional demands on him.

For Karen, of course, it was a different matter. As her feelings for Jay deepened, so did her desire for a permanent, formal relationship. She was aware that Jay was strongly opposed to the idea of marriage, but with her Catholic upbringing it was of great importance to her. As time passed she realized that unless Jay soon changed his outlook, to protect herself she would have to end the affair, however painful that experience might be.

She found a temporary live-in job in a hotel on the other side of the country and announced that she would need a decision from Jay about their future when she returned in two months time. She knew she was taking a huge gamble, but believed that if he really loved her he would miss her and be willing to make a commitment. Fortunately for her the gamble paid off and after only three weeks he phoned with a marriage proposal and pleaded with her to come home at once.

The next obstacle for Karen was her parents' approval—Jay didn't quite fit the bill of their ideal son-in-law. With his unstable family background, lack of steady employment and penchant for gambling, he was clearly unable to offer their daughter the middle-class prosperity she was accustomed to. And although they eventually gave Karen their blessing, they were accurate in their prediction that he would change her life drastically.

They began their marriage in a communal flat which demanded a lot of adjustment on the part of Karen, an only child who had never had to share her belongings. When Jay's travel bug began to bite again, she followed him round Europe, finding hotel work where she could and virtually living out of a suitcase. At the end of their first five years together they had moved home more than a dozen times, before Karen's urge to start a family obliged them to put down some kind of roots and pressurized Jay into finding steady work and taking out a mortgage.

It was partly the stultifying tedium of a nine-to-five white-collar job which drove Jay into an affair with an ex-girlfriend whom he met unexpectedly on business. It was also in part the domestic monotony which arose from the exclusive company of his wife and baby: having never been accustomed to a traditional home life he now found it difficult to come to terms with. He made little attempt to conceal the evidence of the affair, which was really no more than a cry for help. He loved Karen and had no desire to leave her, but what he did need was more space, more time to be himself rather than just a husband or a father.

Regardless of her efforts to tame him, Karen now realized that Jay would always be a free spirit and that unless she allowed him more freedom she—and their child—would surely lose him. By mutual agreement he found a job in the capital where he now lives in a rented apartment five days a week, returning home to his wife and baby at weekends. Despite his complete lack of restriction, Jay now has no interest whatsoever in other women. He looks forward to and immensely enjoys Karen's company and is happy in the knowledge that he has a secure home base to which he can return at will but to which he is not chained.

Although Karen's life is now far different from that which she would have chosen for herself or from that of her own parents, she is surprisingly content with her weekday existence as a single parent and her part-time marriage to Jay. Jay's high wages provide more money for her to spend on leisure activities and babysitters, which has supplied her in turn with more independence. She has come to appreciate being able to do her own thing without the encumbrance or interference of a husband. Yet she is still able to enjoy a sexually and intellectually fulfilling relationship with the man she adores. Indeed their sex-life is better now than it ever was and every weekend is like another honeymoon.

Uranus–Sun

Uranus–Sun cross-aspects are common in romantic relationships which develop very quickly and, in the case of the conjunction, trine and opposition, those which retain their magic right until the end. The galvanizing mutual attraction is based on the ability of both people to awaken each other's zest for living. The Sun seems able to draw out Uranus's eccentricity and encourage him to behave in a more extrovert and uninhibited fashion, whilst even the shyest of Suns can be reassured by unabashed Uranus into moving centre stage and giving a little more of themselves.

The exhilaration generated by this sparkling dual act is so compelling that soon after meeting they may embark on some unconventional course of action. Perhaps they will become involved in some exciting or dangerous work or leisure project, or perhaps they will decide spontaneously to live together. At any rate, with a good karmic contact the Sun may feel that the area of life ruled by her sign placing will soon be thrown into joyful disarray by the antics of Uranus. Uranus in turn can revel in the knowledge that in the Sun he has a partner who will respond to his schemes and dreams, however crazy.

When Uranus plays a positive role he can have a galvanizing influence on the Sun, egging her on to establish her true identity or take the risk of breaking into a more independent or avant-garde lifestyle. Here the Sun can feed off Uranus's confidence, contempt for the status quo and disregard for security, and can be encouraged into experimenting a little for herself.

For the Sun partner whose ego has been inflated by the initial adulation of Uranus, it can be a severe blow to discover that this adulation is neither permanent nor exclusive, that Uranus is also excited by other people and other things, and that she is not always at the epicentre of his universe. In a harmonious relationship the Sun will grudgingly come to terms with Uranus's refusal to worship at her shrine and may find to her surprise that the relationship actually thrives on Uranus's frequent comings and goings, which allow no possibility of monotony or boredom. But when the Sun has challenging karma to meet through the vehicle of Uranus, his inconstancy may be disorientating to her, threatening to her self-esteem and the source of a good deal of pain, at least in the early stages of the relationship.

When Uranus assumes a negative role, it is often because the Sun's all-pervading enthusiasm for her own creativity threatens to swamp him, stifling his own freedom of self-expression. Often Uranus has initially encouraged the Sun's creativity, boosting her sense of achievement and her pride in herself. But the Sun's subsequent assumption that her creative needs will forever take precedence is greeted with outraged horror by Uranus, whose own freedom is always sacrosanct.

Uranus's fear of suffocation may be reinforced by his association of the Sun with a suppressive father-figure from his childhood or a previous life, throwing up memories of past restriction which occurred under similar circumstances. But whatever the root of his fear, Uranus will quickly make it plain to the Sun that he has no intention of being tied down by her ego needs and that her aspirations and ambitions are of little consequence or importance.

Uranus will often make his point by spending increasingly less time with the Sun, thus depriving her of the ego-bolstering feedback on which she was fast becoming dependent. In other cases Uranus will demonstrate his fickleness by verbally ridiculing the achievements and successes of which the Sun is so proud. Now the independence and wit which the Sun originally found so attractive in Uranus are turned ruthlessly against her to cut her down to size and curb her excessive demands.

The Sun does not usually give up without a fight and despite the wounds inflicted by Uranus may try to rekindle his interest and admiration, sometimes by dramatic outbursts and over-the-top behaviour, sometimes by seeking new admirers in a desperate attempt to make him jealous. But all to no avail since, unlike the highly vulnerable Sun, Uranus seemingly has no heart and neither does he have any pride.

Uranus's humiliation of the Sun causes most problems in relationships where the Sun expects to play the dominant role, e.g. of parent or husband, and feels wounded in the absence of sufficient respect. But when the Sun plays the role of wife or child she can often cope better with Uranus's rejection, benefitting from the independence she acquires through Uranus's absences and the emotional detachment she develops in fending off his ridicule.

Sadly there are cases when a Uranus parent's failure to give time to his Sun child or to respect her true identity has a long-term undermining effect on her self-image and sense of security. Or where a Uranus partner's abandonment of a dependent spouse can destroy her emotional or financial stability. But ultimately, if she is to survive, the Sun can only adapt to her compulsory freedom without bitterness and seize the opportunity to become more resourceful and self-determining than would have been possible otherwise. Basically she has no other alternative.

Alan met Susannah when he was working as an up and coming journalist on a left-wing publication and she joined the newspaper as his secretary. The instant chemistry between them was based not only on a strong physical attraction but also on shared socialist leanings and the same adventurous, nonconformist outlook.

Their romance was certainly unconventional, with dates usually spent at some political meeting or demonstration. And because Susannah's parents opposed the match, they eloped when she was just 17 and Alan was 25: in retrospect they decided they did it just for kicks, since marriage wasn't really on either's list of priorities.

But the time finally arrived when they decided to start a family and because Alan was the broodier of the two, it was agreed that he would play an equal part in the child care. What they had not originally envisaged was that Alan would finally take on total responsibility for rearing their son and running the home, assuming the role of house husband, a relatively new phenomenon at that time.

It all came about as a result of a promotion offer which Susannah received from another newspaper shortly before she discovered she was pregnant. It was a rare and long-awaited chance to move up from the typing pool to the rank of junior feature writer. Too good an opportunity, they both agreed, for Susannah to turn down, even if it meant finding a crèche for the baby soon after its birth.

Susannah confirmed with her new employers that she would return to work immediately after her confinement. But as the delivery date drew nearer, Alan became increasingly unhappy about abandoning their child to a stranger and finally announced his intention to take an 18-month sabbatical to research into the mysteries of babycare.

Perhaps it was his Sun in Virgo that gave Alan the aptitude for the well-ordered regime required to keep an infant and its environment clean and tidy. A workaholic at heart, he found it quite easy to turn his diligence to domestic affairs and soon had the household running like clockwork. Perhaps it was Susannah's Uranus in square to his Virgo Sun that brought out this new outlet for his organizational skills, whilst his own Uranus conjunct her Sun in Gemini allowed her the freedom to fulfil her potential as a writer.

It was a role-swap *par excellence*, but even so they had their fair share of arguments, due mainly to Susannah's resentment at seeing so little of her husband. Having been cooped up with the baby all week, Alan liked to spend the weekend playing sport or drinking with former colleagues, which left Susannah on her own, feeling neglected and unloved. She gave him hell when the pressure built up, pouring scorn on his menial status and lack of income, although she would immediately bite her tongue and plead forgiveness. He'd fight back with derisive comments about her job with the right-wing press, taunting her for having abandoned her youthful allegiance to socialism.

The big crisis occurred when Alan's 18-month commitment drew to a close and he began to talk about returning to work and allowing Susannah to experience the joys of motherhood. Not surprisingly, she was hardly bursting with enthusiasm at the idea of relinquishing her independence and tried to pressurize Alan into maintaining the status quo a little longer. But he felt no further obligation to take sole responsibility for their son and made it clear to his wife that the provisions she made for the child were now entirely up to her.

It was far from an ideal arrangement, but when her editor suggested she should work at home as a freelance, Susannah decided it was the best option available to her that satisfied her maternal conscience whilst providing some intellectual stimulation. In effect things worked out better than she had hoped and the new routine she feared would spell the end of her freedom actually opened up many new doors. As a freelance, she had greater scope for creativity, she could work the hours that suited her best and she still had time to enjoy her child.

After a six-month field trip collecting material for a book on the Third World, Alan returned home refreshed and impassioned by the desire to make the planet a better place, reawakening Susannah's commitment to the socialist principles of her youth and making her fall in love with him all over again.

Nowadays they both work from home, Alan as an author and Susannah as a freelance feature writer, and both take their turn with the child care. Occasionally each complains about their unfair share of the chores or of having no life of their own, but on the whole the set-up seems to work fairly well, at least for a two-way Uranus cross-aspect.

Uranus–Moon

When Uranus meets the Moon, the atmosphere is alive with an unmistakable electricity. This is a combination which produces a phenomenal degree of emotional tension, a tension which often has sexual overtones and which in some cases can lead to a magnetic romantic attraction, but in others can be irritating and psychologically exhausting.

The key to the magic is the Moon's ability to put Uranus sufficiently at ease to express the whackier side of his temperament. In the Moon Uranus finds someone who responds instantly to his zany sense of humour, who appreciates his love of the droll and the ridiculous and who encourages and applauds his eccentricities. Uranus effervesces in the company of the Moon and is able to behave spontaneously and unselfconsciously—with the Moon he can let it all hang out without any fear of censure.

Who could resist the sparkling charisma of Uranus? The Moon certainly cannot and may find that Uranus turns her on in ways that no one else can. Uranus has the ability to arouse a level of emotional excitement in the Moon which is sometimes rather dangerous, almost out of control. The Moon often finds that her feelings are switched on and off by Uranus at lightning speed and that one moment she may be laughing, the next crying. All in all Uranus has an emotionally liberating influence on the Moon which often can be delightfully refreshing, especially when she is normally rather fixed in her response.

When a Uranus–Moon contact works well it can result in a gloriously fun-filled relationship based on a shared off-beat humour. It is a relationship which thrives on provocative playfulness—playful teasing and an abundance of witty repartee, with the Moon usually playing the stooge. There is always an element of flirtation in this relationship, at least on the part of Uranus, an urge to wind the other person up just for kicks but to back off quickly when things get heavy.

The adaptability and detachment which form an essential part of this association can often be helpful to the Moon in enabling her to develop greater emotional strength and become less of a victim of her own feelings. The service rendered by Uranus to the Moon is to help her come to terms with change—change of feeling and frequently change of circumstances. Uranus is often successful in bringing a timid Moon out of her shell, encouraging her to expand her range of experience and generally be more sociable. But the assistance is not all one way. Uranus's independence, adventurousness and risk-taking cannot manifest without the love and nurturing of the Moon, and the knowledge that he has her support to fall back on when the going gets tough.

It is a different story when the two people have hard karma to meet in their relationship, in which case the emotional excitement and changeability can be simply too much for the Moon and can even drive her to distraction. Here Uranus's unpredictable mood swings can be incomprehensible and frightening to the Moon and can seriously upset her need for emotional stability. Uranus's highly strung temperament can set the Moon's nerves on edge and his restlessness and lack of domesticity can threaten her dependency on a secure home and family life.

Here Uranus's piquant sense of humour loses much of its playfulness and can be directed against the Moon in a cruel and humiliating way, mimicking her mannerisms, winding her up mercilessly, then poking fun at her hurt feelings. The truth is that although Uranus often feels at liberty to indulge in the most over-the-top behaviour himself, he cannot accept or respond to the Moon's own emotional self-expression without subjecting her to mockery and scorn.

It is this lack of balance which is often hardest for the Moon to come to terms with. As one who gives unreservedly at the emotional level, she must eventually feel cheated by Uranus's lack of tenderness and sensitivity, his coolness and his detachedness. Sooner or later the Moon ends up feeling alone and misunderstood, not knowing whether she is loved or despised by Uranus.

Certainly he is unlikely to express his love for her in conventional terms or to indulge in the schmaltzy displays of affection she often craves.

In reality it is hardly ever the case that Uranus does not have a great deal of love for the Moon, but he is inhibited by deep fears from giving full expression to that love. Uranus's greatest dread is that he may be possessed or imprisoned by his love, and his physical or emotional distancing of the loved one is designed to ensure that this does not happen. The Moon's clinginess and emotional demands can strike terror in the heart of Uranus, as he sees his freedom slowly ebbing away. Her innocent desire to envelop her beloved in a cocoon of love is viewed by him as an attempt at suffocation and must be thwarted at all costs, even at the expense of her delicate feelings. Sometimes Uranus's anxiety is sparked off by subconscious memories of a past-life emotionally stifling relationship with the Moon, or by her resemblance to a mother-figure from his past who made excessive and debilitating emotional demands on him.

With negative karma, Uranus–Moon contacts make for a particularly difficult relationship due to the contrast between Uranus's resistance to emotional commitment and the Moon's hunger for it. Uranus responds only to logic and reasoning, which in the Moon's eyes have no place in love. The Moon can express herself only in emotional language which is incomprehensible to Uranus and merely reinforces his detachment. The ultimate outcome is often a serious communication breakdown between the two players.

The communication problem can be especially hard for a Moon child with a Uranus parent, who is unable to give the child sufficient time and can't empathize with her or approach her on her own terms. Often this is a parent who dislikes kids and the gooey emotions which surround them, and expects to have an intellectual relationship with his child from the age of 2. In the best of cases the Moon child will respond to Uranus's detached approach by growing up to be emotionally robust and independent of her parents at an early age. In the worst of cases she can be deeply scarred by Uranus's derision of her feeling nature, which can adversely affect her ability to trust or show her feelings later in life.

Lee was illegitimate, the result of a casual affair between his mother Liz and a fellow student. Liz had initially decided on an abortion but changed her mind at the last minute, even though it meant abandoning her drama studies and her hopes of a career on the stage. She promised herself she would break into acting later on when the child was older, but somehow it never quite materialized. The waitressing work she took up on a temporary basis was extended indefinitely and the only outlet she found for her love of drama was in her relationships with men, which were numerous, torrid and often traumatic.

Good accommodation was hard to come by for an unmarried mother, and by the time Lee was 5 he had moved home six times, reflected perhaps by his mother's Uranus in opposition to his Moon in Capricorn, a Moon placing which longs for structure and order but is often thrown back on its own resources and obliged to grow up well before its time.

Lee saw little of his mother during his early years. During the week she left him in a day nursery and most evenings she liked to get out. She would have cracked up if she hadn't allowed herself some fun—she'd given up so much already. She couldn't always afford a babysitter and on those occasions she would leave the boy alone in the apartment, convincing herself that he'd sleep right through. But often he was awoken by vivid nightmares, and his screams for his mother were greeted only by the vacant silence echoing in the dark and empty house.

Whenever she was at home, however, Liz was wonderful fun to be with, and when he was a youngster Lee adored her company. She excelled at impersonations of his teachers, which provided great amusement for him and his friends, and she loved to join in with all their games, climbing trees like the tomboy she was at heart. She was nothing like the other mums, more of an older sister than a mother, more of a mate than a parent. Never unduly strict, she actually encouraged him to be a rebel, although in reality he was far from a rebel by nature. Quite the reverse in fact, a shy and conformist type of boy who sometimes wondered, as he grew up, how he had acquired a mother so unlike himself.

If questioned, Liz would always maintain that she had a close and happy relationship with her son. She knew she had little maternal instinct and that she coped with Lee only by treating him as an adult, but she thought he appreciated her acknowledgement of his maturity and her willingness to consider him an equal. He seemed to enjoy her taking him into her confidence—he was always so ready to listen to her problems, calm her down and dry her tears.

What she failed to realize was that the emotional outbursts to which she was frequently prone were disturbing to Lee and made him quietly afraid for his mother's sanity. Neither did she notice that he too would often have liked to confide his troubles in her, but simply never had the chance. Her own problems always took priority, whilst his were dismissed as unimportant, like the time he was being bullied at school and she just laughed it off.

It was after the bullying incident when he was in his early teens that Lee began to question his mother's real concern for him and became more critical of her eccentricities. The desire to fit in with his peers combined with his natural conservativeness made him acutely embarrassed about her unconventional personality and lifestyle. He was reluctant to bring his friends home because he never knew what kind of emotional state he would find Liz in, sometimes in a state of hysteria, sometimes slumped in depression after a romantic tiff.

Occasionally she would prepare a delicious meal for them but more often than not there was no food in the house and she would send him out to buy a take-away. The people she brought back to the apartment got on his nerves too—weird types like her feminist girlfriend with her crewcut and dungarees, the sort of person he wanted nothing to do with and who made him a laughing-stock amongst his mates.

When Lee announced his intention to leave school at 16 to enter the civil service his mother thought he was completely crazy; she would never have chosen such a boring career for him. Soon after starting work he also moved out of his mother's apartment and took board with a working colleague. It had reached the point where he had no privacy or comfort whatsoever at home, the final straw having been the arrival of Liz's latest live-in boyfriend, a long-haired guitarist who spent every day in bed and most nights playing loud music.

Lee knew he'd be better off without his mother, but the parting still hurt and he felt resentful towards her for driving him out of his rightful home. Years later he worked on his anger towards her in therapy and after a long period of little contact now sees her quite often as a pal, which of course was just what she'd always been. Liz herself is just the same, still the drama queen, still oblivious to the pain she inadvertently inflicted on her son. In her eyes they always had, and still have, a simply wonderful friendship.

Uranus–Mercury

The success of relationships involving Uranus–Mercury cross-aspects ultimately depends on whether Mercury is sufficiently robust to handle the provocative and unpredictable statements which flow unceasingly from Uranus. Mercury in an air or fire sign usually enjoys the challenge of ongoing mental stimulation and perhaps a little verbal sparring. But Mercury in earth may not be quick-witted enough to keep up with Uranus's lightning speed of thought, while Mercury in water is often far too sensitive to cope with the sarcastic cut and thrust of Uranus's conversation.

But when this combination works well it provides for an electrifying meeting of minds, which keeps both people mentally on their toes and sharpens their intellect to a fine point. For Uranus there is the excitement of finding in Mercury someone who sparks off his thoughts, who is willing to listen to his more controversial or obscure ideas and who is able to provide him with lively and intelligent feedback. Mercury in turn cannot but be spellbound by Uranus's glittering wit, his daring and original use of words and his courage in broaching risqué subjects.

There is nearly always a good deal of mutual flirtation based on quick-fire verbal exchange. The magnetic attraction always present in Uranus cross-aspects is based here on content and tone of speech, even accent, and it is not uncommon for the two people to fall in love simply with each other's voice, at least initially.

At best these two players are able to expand each other's thinking, albeit in a light-hearted and highly enjoyable way. Uranus encourages Mercury to be a little more open-minded, to speak out a little more fearlessly and perhaps to take up a new line of study. And Mercury can be highly useful to Uranus as a source of factual information which will further broaden his horizons and provide a new angle on intellectual issues. In other cases Mercury can serve as a mouthpiece or scribe for Uranus, able to understand, articulate and record his more abstract ideas.

But the two people are not always receptive to each other's help. When challenging karma abounds, Mercury can be suspicious of Uranus's brashness and uneasy about his outspokenness. Uranus in particular is highly susceptible to subconscious fears, fears that Mercury may curb his independence of thought or put an end to his mental freewheeling, fears which prevent him from accepting the valuable insights that Mercury has to offer. In the attempt to preserve his sense of intellectual superiority, Uranus may set out to make Mercury look stupid, ridiculing the content or delivery of her statements and comments. Frequently he will refuse to be drawn into any meaningful exchange of ideas with Mercury, answering every question with another, challenging almost everything she says and continuously disrupting the conversation flow.

Mercury's natural desire for clear communication is frustrated by the elusive Uranus who, to avoid committing himself, indulges in verbal games which he can pursue for hours without saying anything of significance. Uranus's favourite role is that of devil's advocate, leg-puller, creator of shockwaves, all designed to conceal his true opinions and all highly amusing stuff—but not to Mercury, when she is seeking precise information or is simply in need of a good chat.

Perhaps the most annoying aspect of Uranus's elusiveness is his tendency to change his opinion with staggering frequency, leaving Mercury bewildered at the suddenness of his about-face and his casual dismissal of a previous stance. Faced with unpredictability of this magnitude, it is not surprising that sooner or later Mercury may seriously doubt Uranus's integrity.

There is a fine line between Uranus's playfulness and his deliberate obstructiveness, and it is often difficult for Mercury to complain when Uranus claims to be just joking. But what Uranus is pleased to consider as a joke often appears to Mercury as bloody-minded perversity and may trigger the sharp side of Mercury's tongue, leading to caustic verbal exchanges.

In some cases it is Uranus's association of Mercury with a much-hated teacher from his childhood or a past life which lies at the root of his offhanded approach towards her and his unwillingness to listen to what she has to say. For Mercury the karmic challenge is to learn to think for herself, to reassess her beliefs constantly without relying on Uranus's insights. In effect she can do little else when Uranus is behaving badly, since she will rarely obtain much sense from him at such times.

For a Mercury child with a Uranus mother or father the cross-aspect is something of a mixed blessing. There can be the challenge of developing sufficient dexterity of wit to keep tracks with her parent's lively intellect. There is the opportunity to become acquainted through Uranus with an unusually wide range of subjects and to broaden her horizons beyond those of her peers. But if the child is constantly humiliated by her Uranian parent and made to feel intellectually inferior, the repercussions to her self-esteem can be serious and can lead to inhibited verbal self-expression later on in life.

When John's younger sister Carol was born he went through all the usual sibling jealousy, exacerbated in his case by his mother's obvious preference for girls. Carol soon proved to be all the things he wasn't—delicate and pretty whereas he was fat and ungainly, artistically gifted whereas he was distinctly lacking in imagination. The only asset he possessed which she did not was academic prowess—he was a natural scholar, excelling in the sciences, with the brains and the determination to claim the highest prizes.

John's teasing of his sister began as an effective means of venting his jealousy of her. It was all so easy—with her Mercury in Pisces square to her brother's Uranus, Carol was absent-minded and a little slow on the uptake, making her the perfect target for John's belittling attacks. He could tie her in knots in an argument and never once missed an opportunity to prove his intellectual superiority.

But it wasn't only a question of jealousy. John found Carol's meandering, illogical mind highly irritating, her incessant and meaningless chatter drove him crazy and a sharp verbal put-down was the only way he knew of shutting her up. Despite this she always came back for more, pestering him to tell her a story or play 'make believe' games, or boring him with tedious accounts of books she had read. He complained to his mother that he just didn't have the time to waste and simply wished to be left alone. But perhaps deep inside he feared he might find her magic world a little too fascinating if he looked close enough—and nothing could be allowed to compromise his pragmatic outlook.

Carol's feelings towards John were a complex mixture of love and hate. He was the cleverest person she knew and far from envying him she respected and admired his unlimited knowledge and sharpness of mind. What she did resent, however, was the way he always made her look a fool in public, mystifying her with long and complex words she didn't know or subtle jokes she never understood. She longed to be able to win an argument, just once, to prove to herself she wasn't as dumb as he thought she was, but somehow she never managed it.

As time passed she became increasingly tongue-tied whenever John was around, imagining that he was always watching her, waiting for her to say something stupid. She felt too that he was almost willing her to flunk her exams to confirm his predictions and as usual of course she proved him right. Part of her longed for John to leave home and free her of his taunting sarcasm, but the part of her that loved him dreaded losing him. And sure enough when he passed his finals and took up his place at college she soon came to miss his irrascible company and found life was strangely boring without him.

The parting from his sister had a positive effect on John. It was not until he had left home, returning only during the vacations, that he found he could actually enjoy his sister's company. Perhaps it was because he no longer needed to compete with her for his parents' approval, or perhaps it was because he now had more freedom and could choose when to see her and when not. Certainly he now found Carol more interesting to talk to and although she was just as woolly-headed, just as vague and long-winded, he no longer found her so exasperating. Now, all at once, he began to appreciate her sensitivity and the richness of her imagination, and when she took up astrology he allowed himself to become involved in one of her interests for the first time.

To his surprise he was quickly ensnared and immersed himself in a deep study of astrology with his usual thoroughness and diligence. Of course he soon overtook his sister in his factual knowledge of the subject, but found her inspired insights of great value and interest. Thanks to his sister John has discovered a discipline which suits his scientific approach but also allows for the development of his neglected intuition. And Carol has at last found a topic of mutual interest which she can discuss with John as an equal.

Uranus–Venus

In romantic relationships, this is the classic aspect of love at first sight, of two pairs of eyes meeting across a crowded room, of flashing lights and pounding hearts. It is also the aspect associated with one-night stands, short-lived affairs and fickle changes of heart. This is not to say that the passionate feelings experienced by many people at the start of a Uranus–Venus relationship cannot continue to smoulder indefinitely, but they need careful handling, especially on the part of Venus, if they are not to burn themselves out prematurely.

There can be no hope of long-term harmony unless Uranus is

permitted adequate freedom, for despite his powerful attraction to Venus, the prospect of a permanent or exclusive relationship never figures amongst his plans. For Uranus the thrill is in the chase, not the conquest; his libido is aroused by uncertainty, turned off by security. The trick is to maintain the element of excitement, perhaps by mutually independent lifestyles or perhaps by frequent partings, although sexual infidelity is not necessarily an issue.

More than any other planet, Venus brings out the flirt in Uranus. The beauty and charm which Uranus perceives in Venus are stimulating to him, breaking down his social inhibitions with much the same effect as a few stiff drinks. Venus too is receptive to the sexual chemistry generated through her interaction with Uranus and for both players there can be the expectation of a thrilling love affair, or at least an exciting friendship. Venus, however, may harbour doubts concerning the honourability of Uranus's intentions, fearing he may love her and leave her, due perhaps to Uranus's philandering reputation or to unconscious memories of his past-life unfaithfulness.

Uranus's fickleness is always a potential problem, but is most likely to manifest when he is forced into a suffocating one-to-one relationship with Venus with little outlet for his gregariousness. Social imprisonment can cause Venus's desirability to pall considerably for Uranus and can even drive him away for good, if he feels he is seriously threatened. The problem is that as the relationship develops, Venus expects constant companionship whereas Uranus demands a life of his own; Venus expects Uranus's ardour to burn continuously whereas of its very nature it is highly spasmodic. The more Venus clings, the more Uranus fights to shake himself free, which often manifests as inconsiderate and unkind behaviour towards her. Uranus's stand-offishness is stimulated by a fear of being smothered by Venus's affection, a fear which often has its roots in a past-life experience of this kind.

When Venus has challenging karma to confront in her relationship with Uranus, she may suffer badly through his unwillingness to show any commitment and his tendency to spread his affections around indiscriminately. Uranus's flirtatiousness, once so exciting to Venus, often becomes a source of torment, with Uranus behaving as if he were still single even after having taken marriage vows. It can be a humiliating experience for Venus to witness her lover chatting up others, to be ignored or even personally insulted.

It seems that Venus must often undergo periodic rejection by Uranus, rejection of her sexuality, her desirability and her aesthetic values. The challenge for Venus is to accept that Uranus can still love her despite his occasional lapses and to prove her own love for him by allowing him his freedom.

This can present particular difficulties for Venus when the planet has natal aspects to Pluto or occupies a fixed sign, but if she can learn to live happily with her itinerant lover, he can open many useful doors for her. Given his independence, Uranus can be the most stimulating and delightful of companions, forever helping Venus to discover new ways of having fun, introducing her to new leisure interests or giving her the confidence to exploit an artistic gift. Uranus can also be helpful in dispelling Venus's diffidence and social reserve, widening her circle of friends and bringing exciting new people into her life. And sometimes he may exert a catalytic effect on Venus's finances, which can be either beneficial or disruptive, depending upon her karmic account.

Uranus–Venus is primarily a cross-aspect of romantic attraction, and even when it occurs in child–parent or sibling relationships there is always a magnetic fascination between the two people. A Venus child with a Uranus parent usually enjoys a greater than average amount of social freedom with few restrictions on choice of friends, style of dress or personal expression. But in turn she may have to sacrifice the security of a close and stable parental relationship, since the Uranus parent is frequently absent, either in person or in spirit. The Uranus parent often finds it difficult to relate to feelings and may be unable to respond to the Venus child's expressions of affection, which can be puzzling and hurtful to the youngster. But what it lacks in open demonstrations of love, such a child can often recoup in encouragement to develop its individuality—although unfortunately this is not always so.

When the Uranus parent is out of touch with his own individuality and is scornful of aesthetic values which he cannot personally understand, he may ridicule the Venus child's personal presentation, artistic leanings or sexual preferences when these fail to conform to his own—with grave consequences to a sensitive child.

Conversely the Venus parent with a Uranus child may find she is able to learn much from her offspring, by whom she is kept up to date in terms of social and cultural trends. This is a child who can change his parent's old-fashioned outlook, perhaps through a nonconformist lifestyle or perhaps through an unconventional relationship, forever broadening his Venus parent's horizons and allowing her to remain perpetually young at heart.

It couldn't have happened to a less suitable guy. James, a staunch right-wing broker, had attended a traditional single sex school where any semblance of deviance amongst the boys had been punished by ostracism and where all individuality of self-expression had been effectively suppressed. As a father he had naturally done everything in his power to ensure his children would follow him along the straight and narrow path. So when the indisputable evidence emerged that his son Nick was gay, it seemed to him as if his whole world had been shattered.

Looking back, however, the tell-tale signs had always been there: Nick's striking prettiness as a baby when he was mistaken just a little too often for a girl, his dislike of rough games and early preference for female company, his slightly effeminate gait. But most of all his gloriously camp sense of humour which had always provided such excellent entertainment for everyone, including James—that is until he realized the full implications.

At first James had given every encouragement to his son to develop his off-beat performing skills, paying out good money for drama classes, perhaps because Nick was expressing the rebel in himself which had long since been forced into submission. But later, when Nick simultaneously announced his homosexuality and his plans for a stage career, James's fond indulgence turned to horrified alarm and he immediately withdrew his financial support.

James's ambivalence toward his son arose from his attraction/repulsion for Nick's nonconformism and showmanship, glamorous qualities which secretly excited him because they reflected his unexpressed fifth house Uranus. But because he failed to identify with these qualities and because they had no place in his blinkered reality, he found it difficult to accept their existence in his son and to acknowledge that they could have any worth in society.

It was during his last year at home, before he left to join a repertory company, that Nick bore the full brunt of his father's Uranus square to his own Venus in Aquarius. As James came to terms with his son's defiant rejection of every aspect of his own way of life, regarding both work and relationships, his sense of shock expressed itself in relentless mickey-taking, anti-gay humour and sardonic references to Nick's chosen career as a 'drag artist'. Years later he realized he had been attempting unsuccessfully to make a joke of something he found bewilderingly painful, just as some people feel compelled to laugh instead of cry when confronted with news of a tragedy.

He realized too that he had no other way of expressing the fear he was experiencing, as the world as he knew it was turned upside down. He loved Nick with all his heart, perhaps even more than his other two children. But if he were to show that love, he would also seem to be embracing the unorthodox values which Nick now represented. Saturn, conjunct his Uranus, resurrected his childhood fear of peer disapproval and made him afraid of incurring the contempt of his narrow-minded establishment colleagues if he came out in support of his son.

Although largely unaware of his father's inner turmoil, Nick was surprisingly tolerant of the abuse he received from him. Having realized at an early age that he was different from other boys and would be made to suffer for it, he fell easily into the role of victim. He was well used to being the butt of jokes, although his own father's ridicule was much harder to bear—and to understand.

Deep inside he was certain that James's disaffection was only temporary and that the bond between them was strong enough for him to win back his father's love. He believed also that there was a more liberal side to James which he could bring out, perhaps through his own Uranus in trine to his father's Venus, also in Aquarius like his. Nick was convinced that James had far more in common with him than he had ever cared to admit, such as their shared interest in ecological issues, discovered during long one-to-one discussions when Nick was a little younger and less of a threat.

The turning-point in their relationship was their joint application for membership of an ecological pressure group, which James grudgingly had to admit confirmed a fairly 'alternative' attitude on his part. Gradually the gulf between father and son has lessened and James has come to realize that in order to keep in touch with Nick he will have to become more acceptant of his lifestyle . . . and his boyfriends. Nick is still working on his father and James has at last begun to work a little on himself, trying to break through the inbuilt, senseless prejudice which has robbed him of so much of the fun and enjoyment his relationship with Nick has to offer.

Uranus–Mars

The mutually energizing effect of this, the most power-packed of all the karmic cross-aspects, can bring out the best or the worst of the physical resources of the two people involved. When they are in tune with each other's energy flow they can have a dynamic effect on one another, each encouraging the other towards greater experimentation, independence and assertiveness. But when their karma spells problems, there can be a basic inability to co-operate and a dramatic clash of wills, leading to explosive and sometimes violent arguments and rows.

The physical attraction can be immediate and transfixing. For Uranus there is the thrill of identifying with an aspect of his own individuality in Mars's drive and enthusiasm. There is the possibility that Mars might be someone willing to act out his eccentricities and put his grand schemes into effect, someone who could spark off his crazy imagination. The zest for life which Uranus perceives in Mars is a huge turn-on and appeals to his unquenchable thirst for danger and excitement.

Mars too feels exhilarated by Uranus's company, in particular by the sense that Uranus is the kind of person who will keep her constantly on her mettle, who can't be pushed around and who she won't easily be able to dominate. The challenge to gain control is irresistible to Mars and arouses a powerful urge to impose her will on Uranus, often manifesting as a no-holds-barred attempt at sexual conquest.

In romantic relationships sexuality is always an important element of the attraction and forms a vital outlet for the explosive energy which the two people co-generate. Here the characteristic mutual incitement towards daring behaviour expresses itself in that Mars stimulates Uranus's appetite for sexual innovation, whilst Uranus has an arousing effect on Mars's desires. It makes for a red-hot sex-life in which anything goes and in which the couple can positively express their passionate feelings for each other.

It is always important to find a healthy channel for the turbulent energy flow produced by Uranus–Mars interaction. Bedroom olympics provides one form of therapy, but so can any other form of joint sporting activity provided it includes an element of risk and excitement. The violent confrontations for which this cross-aspect is notorious are most likely to arise when no such tension outlet is available.

When pent-up tensions finally become uncontainable, a Mars–Uranus couple can become seriously dangerous to one another. The tendency of each to break down the other's inhibitions, which at best has such a liberating influence on their sex-life, can also lead to uncontrolled verbal and physical attacks, rash and reckless actions and senseless destruction.

Mars and Uranus are ideally suited to whip up each other's anger. Uranus, fearing he may be coerced by Mars's forcefulness into abandoning his independence of action, may wilfully go his own way, often at Mars's expense and often with serious disruption of Mars's ambitions and plans. Commonly Uranus's fears are invoked by his unconscious recall of an earlier relationship in which an authority-figure closely resembling Mars deprived him of his physical freedom—or even his life.

Mars in turn may feel she is being pushed around by Uranus's inconsiderate behaviour and will respond, true to character, with outraged fury, perhaps in the form of an impassioned outburst or perhaps by a renewed attempt to force Uranus into submission. But whatever her tactics, Mars has little hope of making headway with Uranus, since he yields neither to emotional nor physical pressure and eventually may turn on Mars with a monstrous and terrifying rage which makes Mars's temper appear quite mild by contrast.

In general, however, Uranus rarely loses his cool, except when pushed to the limit by Mars's authoritarian attitude. Neither does he attempt to exert any control over Mars, regardless of her pushiness. All Uranus desires is to be left to his own devices, not easy however for the hyperactive Mars who finds it all but impossible to let things be. But if she is to break her karmic bondage to Uranus, Mars must be prepared to give Uranus his freedom and cease trying to direct his life. For this to happen, Mars needs to learn to burn off her own energy and find an independent outlet for her drive without constantly imposing it on Uranus.

When each person is prepared to give the other sufficient space, this pair can make a great team in which Uranus thinks up the ideas and Mars puts them into action. Mars in particular can benefit from Uranus's invigoration to overcome her energy blocks and try out new kinds of activities in the area of life ruled by the planet's sign placing.

The animating effect which Uranus exerts on Mars can be particularly beneficial to a Mars child, whose Uranus parent rejects the standard, over-protective nurturing role and gives his offspring sufficient independence to develop courage, nerve and physical resourcefulness. But a Uranus parent may also feel resentful of the Mars child's demands on his freedom, is more likely than most parents to feel imprisoned by his child and may behave unpredictably when pressure builds up. This is the kind of parent who may periodically scream and shout at his child to relieve the tension, or who may walk out one day as a final gesture of rebellion.

In the case of a Mars parent and a Uranus child it is the child who is prone to rebelliousness, which can pose particular problems during his teenage years, especially if Mars uses force in the attempt to discipline her errant offspring. Marked self-restraint is required on the part of Mars to prevent the tragic but all too common situation of the runaway Uranus child, who can no longer endure the aggressive interference of an over-controlling parent.

> Craig could have been a doctor of medicine—he had the brains and the scientific qualifications but decided instead to enter industrial research, which he believed would bring him better material rewards. With Mars in Virgo he was a workaholic and fitness fanatic with little time for frivolity in his life, an approach which had brought him professional success but had destroyed his first marriage, which ended in divorce.
>
> When he met Lucy through a dating agency it was her carefree outlook on life, so different to his own, that he found most intriguing. She had a job as a freelance textile designer, which she thoroughly enjoyed but which never got in the way of her leisure interests. She was involved in many New Age activities such as yoga and healing, subjects which had always interested Craig but for which he had never quite found the time.
>
> With her Uranus square to his Mars, Lucy had a marked loosening up effect on Craig and was the first woman since his wife who was successful in dragging him away from the lab or the gym. But more than anything, it was the powerful sexual attraction he felt for Lucy that caused Craig to fall heavily in love and to his astonishment he found himself suggesting marriage just two short weeks after meeting her.
>
> Lucy too was stunned by the proposal. Since her own divorce she had been reluctant to commit herself to another relationship and was looking merely for friendship, and if possible good sex. She had great respect for Craig's diligence, enjoyed helping him to spend the financial rewards, and found him a thoughtful and exciting lover. But she had no doubt that their affair would be short-lived—apart

from their sexual compatibility they had so little in common.

Having resolved to break things off with Craig before he got hurt, Lucy discovered to her dismay that she was pregnant. Her instinct was still to end the relationship and bring up the child on her own, but when she was eight months pregnant, depressed and helpless, she finally yielded to Craig's pressure and agreed to marry him.

Despite her good intentions, the feeling that fate had played a dirty trick on her made it difficult for Lucy to feel contented in the marriage. With no job, no cash and only the baby for company, she felt she had lost all her independence and although she never voiced the thought, she blamed Craig for making a prisoner of her. Craig too was conscious of the unspoken accusation, sensing that Lucy was with him only because of the baby, not because she loved him, and that like his first wife she too might soon tire of him and walk out.

Perhaps it was because of his emotional insecurity that Craig became increasingly demanding of Lucy, expecting her to keep the house spotlessly tidy and to have his dinner waiting every night— tasks that Lucy, badly organized and hating routine, was ill-suited and unwilling to fulfil. He also began to ask for daily sex, whereby it soon lost its magic for her and became yet another duty.

She came to feel she was nothing other than a housekeeper and a whore, a domestic and sexual slave employed by Craig to do his bidding. Her lifelong hatred of authority, which had led to her expulsion from high school, gave rise to a deep revulsion at her enforced imprisonment and a determination to assert her independence before it was finally too late.

She had always found it difficult to be a good housewife, but now she would deliberately 'forget' to restock the fridge or to iron Craig's shirts. And she would often leave him to look after the baby without due warning, forcing him to cancel his beloved sporting engagements. Eventually she also went on sexual strike, refusing to make love when she didn't want to and sometimes even when she did, just to show him who was boss.

It was the sexual conflict that marked the beginning of the end. When Lucy became frigid Craig felt unloved, for sex had been their only emotional outlet and they had no other way of expressing their affection for each other. Lucy's domestic neglect also made Craig feel uncared for and increasingly afraid of losing her, a fear which expressed itself in his relentless fault-finding which always homed in on her most vulnerable weaknesses and to which she could find no response other than to smash the nearest object.

As their communication deteriorated, Lucy complained that

Craig always side-stepped the source of her discontent, her fundamental sense of isolation, focusing instead on petty domestic conflicts which merely incited her wrath. Craig's main grievance was that Lucy was incapable of logically discussing their difficulties without losing her cool and behaving like a mad woman. He found it difficult to forget their bitter arguments, brooding for days afterwards and suffering from gastric upsets, while she could carry on as if nothing had happened.

They both realized they had reached the end of the road when Craig ended up in hospital after one particularly violent row. He had severed an artery trying to stop Lucy from breaking every window in the house—and all in front of their bewildered and distraught baby daughter. For the child's well-being—and for their own safety—they had to admit they just couldn't live together and they agreed to a trial separation which has continued indefinitely.

Craig has not found it easy to come to terms with the ending of the marriage and vents his resentment of Lucy by scrutinizing her maintenance claims and demanding detailed accounts of her spending. Despite this, Lucy has no hard feelings and now has the detached relationship with Craig that she originally desired. As a single mother she has sacrificed her social and financial independence. But she feels that at least she has retained her sanity, which she once feared she was losing when she was married to Craig.

THE KARMIC
CROSS-ASPECTS OF NEPTUNE

Neptune–Ascendant

The love symbolized by Neptune cross-aspects is that described in the classic romantic novel. It is the kind of love men give their lives for, that inspires acts of self-sacrifice of all kinds. It has a transcendental quality which sets it above mere carnal attraction and is based on a meeting of souls, of seeing one's own divinity reflected in the beloved and of feeling a sense of at-oneness with them.

In Neptune relationships we often fall in love with love, with the state of rapturous bliss we experience when we feel ourselves to be part of another human being. We fall in love not so much with the other person as an individual, as with the emotions generated by our interaction with them. In a sense we are falling in love with ourselves, with our own spiritual beauty which we perceive in the loved one and which is symbolized by a planet or angle of their chart which combines with our Neptune placing.

In Neptune–Ascendant cross-aspects it is the physical appearance of the Ascendant individual which seems so delightfully familar to Neptune and triggers his sense of having found himself. There is a reverent admiration of the Ascendant player's body and self-presentation which is basically devoid of lust, even in sexual partnerships. There is a gentleness and purity to Neptune's feelings for the Ascendant player, an awareness that this is someone very beautiful and very special whom he must treat with great tenderness and care. Without realizing it, Neptune begins to set the Ascendant player on a pedestal, to exaggerate her good points and ignore her bad points and to imbue her with virtues she may not possess.

To be idolized in this way is flattering and elating for the Ascendant player. She feels good when Neptune is around her, basking in the warmth and security of his empathetic presence. She may be mesmerized by the other-worldly mystique irradiated by Neptune, who in turn is transported to another plane by the spiritual rapport he experiences with the Ascendant player. The scene is set for a relationship based on idealization, a relationship which appeals to the two people's loftiest dreams but which may not always be rooted in reality.

Neptune's tendency to make a god out of the Ascendant player often has an important karmic purpose. It can be connected with the karmic service he has chosen to render to her in terms of raising her ideals and enhancing her spirituality. By focusing on the beauty inherent in the Ascendant player, Neptune promotes the manifestation of that beauty. The Ascendant player is often encouraged by Neptune to develop an interest in the arts, in mysticism, or in altruistic activities as a means of getting in touch with her inspirational faculties. Telepathy can develop between the two people as Neptune lifts the consciousness of the Ascendant player onto a non-material plane, although sometimes this can have a spacing-out effect on her, which leads to communication difficulties.

The extent to which Neptune can be successful in 'ennobling' the Ascendant player is dependent on the soundness of his own ideals. It may be that Neptune is someone who finds it hard to reconcile his dreams with hard facts, who attempts to blot out the pain of his disillusionment by self-delusion and escapism. If so, he may also find it hard to see the relationship as it really is, to face its challenges square on, or to be honest with himself or in his dealings with the other person, with resultant disappointment on both sides.

The Ascendant player may sometimes sense that Neptune has some kind of let-down in store for her, or that the relationship will turn out to be other than it initially seemed. But despite her doubts she may proceed regardless, hypnotized by Neptune's subtle magnetism or driven on by a karmic compulsion to suffer the betrayal of her ideals.

When the Ascendant player has challenging karma to undergo in her relationship with Neptune, she will meet with a mirror image of her own maladjusted idealism by falling victim to

Neptune's delusions, delusions which stem from his fear of facing reality and which may be triggered by the Ascendant player's resemblance to someone who betrayed him in the past. Now Neptune seeks to protect himself by creating a false fantasy image of the relationship and refusing to accept any aspect thereof which fails to conform to that fantasy.

Neptune invariably perceives the Ascendant player as he wishes to see her rather than as she really is. He often perceives her as an extension of himself, projecting upon her attitudes and qualities associated with the sign placing of the planet in his chart. Above all he tends to remain strangely blind to her human failings, those unattractive traits which distinguish her as an ordinary mortal to everyone except himself. Until Neptune awakens from his fallacy, he views the Ascendant player as a near-angelic being who must be protected at all costs from the unpleasant side of life.

It is Neptune's desire to spare the supposedly delicate feelings of the Ascendant player that is responsible for his chronic dishonesty in his relationship with her. In the mistaken assumption that he can predict the reactions of the Ascendant player, Neptune may tend to withhold information or to bend the truth slightly so as not to incur her displeasure. But what begins as just 'white lies' can soon develop into a complex web of deceit from which Neptune cannot easily extricate himself and from which one day he may feel compelled to escape—perhaps by suddenly disappearing from the Ascendant player's life.

Neptune's over-idealism is also observable in his unrealistic expectations of himself, which often cause him to feel inadequate in the relationship and to blame himself when things go wrong. Sometimes he will suffer from a permanent sense of guilt or unworthiness of the Ascendant player's love, feelings which can cause him to make a doormat of himself in the relationship as a means of expiation. Neptune's characteristic sense of guilt is aroused perhaps by the Ascendant player's resemblance to someone from his distant past, whom he believes he may have wronged in some way.

Neptune the martyr excels in putting himself down in a number of different ways. Most commonly he will exhaust himself by excessive service to the Ascendant player, exposing himself to exploitation when his partner is of a manipulative bent. But his self-belittlement can also manifest as an inability to make his needs known to the Ascendant player, to assert himself or to give criticism when he feels he is being treated unfairly. By failing to give clear feedback to the Ascendant player he actually invites abuse, since often she is genuinely unaware of Neptune's discontent and resentment. Neptune's continued self-victimization invariably takes a cruel toll on his self-esteem to the point that he can do no other than find an escape route. Here again the Ascendant player may awake one morning to find that Neptune has done a disappearing act.

In other cases it is the relationship itself which forms the focus of Neptune's inability to face reality. Frequently he will envisage the relationship as something that manifestly it is not, misinterpreting the Ascendant player's responses and imagining her to feel more—or less—affection for him than she does in reality. When taken to extremes this can result in an obsessive, one-sided infatuation on the part of Neptune towards the Ascendant player, or perhaps a persecution complex. Neptune's distorted perception of the potential of the relationship can also manifest as false self-representation, where he misleads the Ascendant player as to the true nature of his intentions without ever realizing the confidence trick he is pulling.

But Neptune the confidence trickster must eventually be unmasked and often with tragic consequences for himself and the Ascendant player. The Ascendant player can experience a devastating sense of betrayal when Neptune's lies and deceptions eventually come to light or when a panic-stricken Neptune, threatened with exposure, walks out without explanation leaving behind a legacy of intrigue. The Ascendant player can also feel let down simply by the change in attitude towards her by Neptune, which occurs when he finally sees her as she really is and begins to treat her as an ordinary human being instead of some kind of deity. The confused Ascendant player may wonder what she has done to offend Neptune, when all that has happened is that the rose-tinted spectacles at last have fallen from his eyes.

When the Ascendant player is working through challenging karma, sooner or later she must face the hard fact that her relationship with Neptune is not what she originally thought it was. When the crisis occurs, she may succeed in persuading Neptune to adopt a more honest and realistic approach to the relationship to prevent further disenchantment. She may succeed in helping him to find a creative outlet for his confused idealism, perhaps in the form of artistic activities in which they can participate together. And finally she may help him to accept her and himself and the relationship with all their respective imperfections in an expression of unconditional love.

The Ascendant player can herself express unconditional love towards Neptune by forgiving all past deceits and betrayals and letting go of all grudges. Of course, if Neptune persists in his dishonesty, the Ascendant player may well feel unable to continue living with him. But her forgiveness of him is still essential if she is to avoid a repeat run of the difficulties of the relationship in a forthcoming incarnation.

Larry had always been an obsessive type. From the time he was a teenager he had suffered from painful crushes on girls who were unable to return his feelings, which found an outlet only in his fantasies. His relationship with his wife had been happy at first but was eventually destroyed by his irrational jealousy. At the age of 32 he was alone and depressed, resentful of his ex-wife for her rejection of him, but still in love with her and still believing she would return to him one day, although she hadn't been in touch for more than two years.

He spent most of his time in solitary pursuits, reading or listening to his hi-fi, although once a week he attended the local amateur operatic society and it was here that he came to meet Debbie. She was a classical music buff like himself, sympathetic and so easy to talk to that he felt he had always known her. Debbie was happily married to Paul, but experienced an instant rapport with Larry who seemed to reflect her own feelings on just about everything. There was no question of any romantic interest on her part, she just appreciated his gentleness and warmth and felt totally relaxed in his company. She was also a little sorry for him because he seemed so alone and vulnerable, and she hoped that she and Paul could befriend him.

Paul got on well with Larry at first, sensing no threat from him as a rival since he seemed curiously asexual. It was for this reason that he raised no objections when Larry announced he had two tickets for a concert and asked whether Debbie could accompany him. With three personal planets in Aquarius Paul was not the jealous type and was happy for his wife to enjoy the friendship of other men. The concert outing was a great success and became the first of many over the next few months.

Debbie too was delighted at the opportunity to enjoy some male company other than that of her husband and without the risk of any sexual complications. Larry was so different to Paul—slight in build, cultured and highly sensitive, whereas Paul was a butch outdoor type. Larry gave her a refined, intuitive male perspective on life which she had rarely met with before. He aroused her interest in things esoteric and took her to the spiritualist church, where a gifted medium relayed some poignant messages from her dead father. She was fascinated by the new dimension Larry had introduced into her life, symbolized by his Neptune conjunct her Ascendant, and she continued to enjoy his company, until Paul suddenly became uneasy about the relationship.

Paul's suspicions were first alerted by the increasing number of phone-calls from Larry which would keep Debbie talking for an hour or more. But it was when Paul's squash partner took him aside one evening to put him wise to the rumour, started by Larry himself, that he and Debbie were in love, that he knew without doubt that things had got out of hand.

Debbie was just as shocked as Paul at this distortion of the facts, especially as she had never once considered that Larry might be emotionally involved. She was also angry at Larry for smearing her reputation and for the humiliation she felt he had brought to Paul. But despite her outrage, when she broke the news to Larry that their friendship was over she was surprisingly gentle and was overcome by a huge surge of pity towards him. He struck such a pathetic figure, begging her forgiveness with tears welling up in his eyes—extraordinary behaviour, she thought, for a man of his age, more like that of a love-struck teenager. She was also rather frightened by his unrelenting devotion and his inability to accept that there was no romance between them. For the first time she began to fear for her safety, and she knew it would be impossible for her ever to see him again.

Larry found it hard to accept the finality of Debbie's decision, preferring to believe she had ended the relationship only under pressure from her husband. He wrote desperate, reproachful letters to Paul, accusing him of ruining his life and threatening suicide. He hung around outside their home for hours on end, hoping to catch a glimpse of Debbie and persuade her to change her mind.

When Debbie continued to refuse to speak to him, Larry's resentment finally transferred itself from Paul to her, his obsessional love transmuting into obsessional hatred and a neurosis that she had deliberately set out to destroy him. He came to believe that the whole town was laughing at him behind his back, withdrawing increasingly into himself until finally he suffered a nervous breakdown.

It took Larry two years to get over his fixation with Debbie, although even now he is still convinced that she did love him once. Debbie has learnt the importance of controlling her feelings of pity and making her position towards the opposite sex ultra-clear. With a Neptune–Mercury square in her natal chart, clarity of communication had never been her strong point.

Neptune–Sun

A cross-aspect to the Sun provides Neptune with the perfect outlet for his urge to give all to the loved one, since the Sun thrives on adulation and accepts it greedily. If Neptune's idealism is reasonably well balanced, this can be a mutually elevating combination which promotes both players' ability to express themselves creatively. But if Neptune's perception of the Sun is based more on fantasy than fact, his irrational idolization eventually can have a disastrous effect on the relationship, undermining any love the two people first felt for each other.

The bond of attraction between Neptune and the Sun arises from the intuitive rapport experienced by Neptune with the Sun's self-expression. Neptune closely identifies with the ambitions, talents and successes of the Sun, which he feels to be almost part of himself or at any rate symbols of his own wistful desires. At least in the early stages of the relationship Neptune has nothing but admiration for the Sun's desire to gain recognition and believes her to be capable of no wrong.

For the Sun there is normally a feeling of close kinship with Neptune, a delight in his willingness to share in her achievements, console her when her pride is wounded and provide empathetic, supportive feedback. Above all, the Sun feels able to relax totally with Neptune, to be herself—however uninhibited—without fear of criticism or competition.

Each of these two planets has something of value for the other. From Neptune the Sun receives the motivation to express herself with greater sensitivity and intuition in her chosen area of self-expression. Neptune in turn can be assisted by the Sun to make more creative use of his finer feelings and gain the confidence to translate his hopes and dreams into reality. For this reason the two people often can work successfully together in joint artistic ventures, sometimes on a professional or sometimes on a leisure basis.

But Neptune is not simply sweetness and light and his seeming devotion to the Sun is not always exactly what it appears. Neptune, the master of delusion, can deceive both himself and the other person as to his true feelings in the relationship, usually due to a subconscious unwillingness to confront the pain of disappointment. Often Neptune is reminded by the Sun of a father-figure from his past who let him down or violated his trust and from whom he now seeks to protect himself. As always escapism is Neptune's chosen means of self-defence, permitting him to shut out from his awareness anything about the Sun or his relationship with her likely to reawaken his pain.

In other cases the Sun bears a strong resemblance to an individual Neptune believes he may have wronged, either earlier in his present life or perhaps in a past life. It may even be that the Sun is the reincarnation of the wronged individual, giving rise to feelings of self-blame on the part of Neptune and unrealistic demands of himself to expiate his guilt.

Neptune's excessive expectations of himself, of the Sun and of their relationship with each other can create a bubble of illusion, doomed eventually to burst in mutual disenchantment. Neptune's over-idealized perception of the Sun as confident, creative and authoritative may soon degenerate into a more accurate view of her as vain, proud and dictatorial. When Neptune has fed false hopes to the Sun or has withheld facts from her for fear of injuring her pride, the eventual disclosure of the truth can prove shattering to her faith in Neptune and more devastating to her self-esteem than original honesty. When Neptune has slavishly devoted himself to the Sun's self-expressive needs, sooner or later he may tire of constantly putting himself last and seek some form of escape from her demands.

The Sun's outrage at Neptune's desertion of her is based on genuine shock at his apparent betrayal and the withdrawal of the hero-worship to which she felt fully entitled. Rarely will she question her own collusion in Neptune's self-delusion, which arises from her vision of herself as the centre of the universe.

The Sun's exploitation of Neptune's guilt-ridden self-sacrifice can be especially detrimental in a parent–child relationship, where a dominating, ageing Sun parent allows a subservient

Neptune child to relinquish his own happiness in life in order to satisfy her need for constant attention. On the other hand, a Neptune child can make equally unreasonable demands on a Sun mother or father, setting impossible-to-meet parental standards and criticizing the Sun parent for her inadequacy as a role model.

When the roles are reversed, a Neptune parent is often of the type who idolizes his Sun child, imagining her to be gifted beyond her true capabilities and projecting onto her his own unfulfilled creative ambitions. This places a crippling burden on the Sun child, obliging her to strive for the recognition expected by her parent and to cope with his disappointment when she fails to live up to his dream. The besotted Neptune parent can also exert unreasonable pressure on his Sun child by making extreme self-sacrifices to finance the development of her talents and then reproaching her for her lack of gratitude.

But whatever the nature of the relationship, the challenges to both players in this cross-aspect are basically identical. Whatever Neptune gives to the Sun he is called upon to give to her freely and unconditionally and without bemoaning her insensitivity and thanklessness. The Sun too is called upon to love Neptune unconditionally by expressing forgiveness of his evasiveness, his deceitfulness and his attempts to make her feel guilty—at least if she wishes to sever her karmic bondage.

Gary was from a working-class background and had left school early to begin an apprenticeship in carpentry. Amanda had fulfilled her middle-class parents' ambitions for her by winning a college scholarship, graduating and taking a job as a schoolteacher. An unlikely match, one might imagine, but when Gary and Amanda met at a film club they were immediately drawn to each other as kindred spirits.

Amanda was nothing like the other educated women Gary had met in the past, whom he had found to be rather snobbish. Never once did he feel inferior or out of place in Amanda's company, never once did she treat him patronizingly. Perhaps it was their shared love of fantasy that forged a bond between them which transcended the barriers of social or intellectual status. Certainly, despite the limited things they had in common, as their love affair developed, each appeared to blossom and even to undergo a personality transformation.

Amanda had always been a bluestocking, with little interest in her appearance and decidedly reserved in temperament. Yet under Gary's influence she appeared to metamorphose into a vivacious and attractive woman, who became the centre of attention in any room she entered. Even her own family found it hard to recognize the new Amanda and found it even harder to believe that, at Gary's suggestion, she planned to set up her own kindergarten school. Although this had been a lifelong dream, she had been held back by her basic lack of self-belief, which now took a giant leap forwards as a result of Gary's constant attention and flattery.

Gary too found a new confidence in himself which allowed him to contemplate putting into action some of his long-held ambitions, which as yet had been no more than figments of his imagination. He had always wanted to travel or even live overseas, yet had always lacked the energy or the self-assurance to make the necessary arrangements. But with her natural organizing ability Amanda was soon setting up joint holidays in Europe and even helping him to obtain a work permit which would enable him to obtain a job abroad.

There is no doubt that without Amanda's encouragement Gary would never have obtained the contract for 12 months carpentry work in Canada and he was grateful to her for her help. What he had not envisaged was that she intended to accompany him in order to set up her school there—and to continue organizing his life *ad infinitum.*

He liked her tremendously and had great admiration for her dynamic ability to get things done. But he was also unnerved by her pushiness, and her detailed plans for their future together; his natal Uranus in opposition to Amanda's Sun urged him to beat a hasty retreat, but his natal Neptune in square to her Sun made it difficult for him to do so openly. He came to a compromise with himself by suggesting to Amanda that he travel alone to Canada to prove his self-reliance and that she should follow on later when he was established. And maybe Gary would indeed have sent for her, if he had not fallen in love with another girl soon after his arrival in Canada.

Had he wished, the new romance could have provided the perfect excuse for ending his relationship with Amanda, but their Neptune–Sun cross-aspect, exacerbated by a Neptune–Mercury conjunction in his own chart, made him too much of a coward to tell her the truth. He was certainly aware that he ought to own up about his new girlfriend, especially after they moved in together, but whenever he put pen to paper he seemed struck dumb, at a loss for the right words to break the news. Even Amanda's announcement that she had booked a flight and would be visiting him for a month couldn't galvanize him into honesty. He hoped that by careful manoeuvring he would be able to keep the two females' existence from each other and find some excuse to postpone Amanda joining him permanently. Although he loved his new girlfriend he was still very fond of Amanda and sincerely believed he was acting in both women's best interests.

When things were finally over between them, Amanda was bitterly derisive of Gary's professed good intentions. She felt, not without good reason, that he had deliberately deceived her and made a fool of her, that his lying had wasted a precious 12 months of her life. It was not in fact until her second visit to Canada, almost exactly one year after Gary's departure, that she at last learned of the existence of his girlfriend—who by then was three months pregnant and anxious for Gary to marry her.

Prior to this, letters had continued to arrive from Gary, perhaps less frequent than before, perhaps less openly affectionate, but giving no reason to believe that he had lost interest or found someone new. His letters talked of his search for premises for her new school and unbelievably he had even promised to buy her an engagement ring. Amanda simply couldn't understand why Gary had misled her so cruelly—was he a pathological liar or simply too weak and frightened to say no to her?

As she struggled to come to terms with the ending of the relationship, Amanda's predominant emotion was that of confusion. It now seemed that Gary had never loved her and that he had only ever gone along with her plans in order to appease her. Yet from their very first meeting he had always led her to believe that he cared deeply for her and she had never once doubted that one day they would be wed. Since Gary disappeared for good from her life, Amanda has reverted to her former introverted self. Her career once again is the main focus in her life and she rarely attends social events, not even the cinema.

Neptune–Moon

The profound empathy that can exist between two people with this cross-aspect allows them instant receptivity to the other's emotions. Especially on the part of Neptune there can be the ability to tune into the Moon's feelings almost before she herself is aware of them, rather as a mother will awake just before her baby begins to cry.

There is much of the idealized mother–child relationship in any contact based on this cross-aspect: a close, often psychic rapport, tender unselfish love, a refusal to think badly of the loved one, and sometimes self-sacrifice. Even in sexual relationships Neptune–Moon love is of a pure, untainted character; it signifies a union which goes beyond the physical and whose karmic function is often to transform the spiritual values of the two people. Indeed, Neptune has often chosen to enact a karmic service to the Moon by offering her unlimited, unconditional love which inspires her in turn to refine her own feelings.

However, the quality of Neptune's service to the Moon is governed by his personal capacity to ground his ideals, to relate at the material level as well as the spiritual and to come to terms with the real shortcomings in others and in himself. Unless Neptune is willing to love all aspects of himself, including his darkness, he will be unable to express unconditional love for the Moon. Unless he can acknowledge and accept all of his feelings, including the more negative ones, he will be unable to achieve a full and honest emotional rapport with the Moon. Where Neptune is accustomed to focusing only on his 'acceptable' emotions, he is likely to falsely perceive the Moon as a much 'nicer' person than she is in reality, an illusion which is in no way helpful to the Moon and can eventually give rise to much heartache.

Neptune's difficulty in perceiving the true temperament of the Moon may also be brought about by the Moon's close resemblance to a female figure from his past, often a mother, with whom he experienced a deeply painful relationship, too painful perhaps to acknowledge. By creating a perfect fantasy image of his relationship with the Moon, Neptune attempts to protect himself from unpleasant memories of the past.

Neptune's service to the Moon may well be entirely without self-interest—an altruistic gesture in gratitude for the Moon's help in previous incarnations. But in other cases it is motivated more by guilt over his emotional mistreatment of the Moon in a past life— or perhaps of an individual who Neptune subconsciously associates with the Moon. The urge to do penance now causes Neptune to endeavour at all costs to avoid upsetting the Moon's feelings, even if in so doing he must conceal his own hurt feelings or make a doormat of himself. This self-denigration on the part of Neptune is also detrimental to the Moon, since the deception and lack of balance which arises in the relationship can lead eventually to its destruction.

When a Neptune–Moon relationship fails, it is often to the complete surprise of the Moon, who may have had no idea that anything was wrong. Often it is not until Neptune withdraws emotionally from the relationship that the Moon becomes aware of his sense of emotional exploitation and hidden resentments. Because it is so difficult for Neptune to express his grievances openly to the Moon, it is important for the two people to establish from the start a pattern of mutual feedback which is clear and honest. It is helpful if the Moon can remain alert to and discourage Neptune's deviousness and self-denial, can urge him to discharge his feelings of disillusionment and can provide him with stable emotional support.

When this is impossible, the relationship is often marred by mutual misunderstandings in which each person feels they have been emotionally betrayed by the other. It is common for Neptune, on awaking to an accurate perception of the Moon's less attractive emotional make-up, to believe that she has turned against him. The Moon in turn can feel horribly let down by the dissolution of Neptune's seemingly boundless love and at Neptune's suggestion may herself take the blame for his sudden change of affection. Neptune excels in inducing powerful feelings of guilt—both in himself and in others.

The two-way guilt-trip is especially manifest in parent–child relationships in which a Neptune parent who blames himself unreasonably for his Moon child's emotional distress may subsequently cause the child to feel guilty about her parent's self-torment. The Neptune parent finds it extremely difficult to detach himself from the Moon child's feelings, and as a result can be stiflingly over-protective towards her.

A Neptune child can likewise over-identify with a Moon parent's emotional state, experiencing excessive concern for his ageing mother or father's happiness and often abandoning his own chances of happiness in service to his parent. But the Neptune child is also capable of assuming the role of the perpetually discontented, never-satisfied offspring, who accuses his Moon parent of inadequate nurturing and love.

When the Moon faces hard karma in her relationship with Neptune, she may suffer considerably from Neptune's unjustified criticism and emotional inconstancy. It can be a shattering experience to be treated one day as a god but the next as a devil, and the Moon is called upon to summon up all her powers of understanding and forgiveness. Attunement to unconditional love is indeed the spiritual purpose of this relationship and what both people have to learn from their interaction with each other. In some cases the Moon must learn this lesson the hard way, but in others a good Neptune can bring out the best in the Moon gently and easily, simply by example. At his best Neptune will also draw out the inspirational qualities of the Moon, helping her to give artistic or spiritual expression to her feelings in creative activities.

Pamela had always longed for a baby sister so when little Rosie was born she immediately became the focus of the elder girl's lavish affections. At 6 years of age Pamela was past the point of sibling jealousy and felt nothing but fascinated delight in the baby's happy smile and outgoing disposition. In Pamela's eyes Rosie was the most adorable little sister who had ever been born, a view symbolized astrologically by Pamela's Neptune in conjunction with Rosie's Moon in Libra.

But with Moon semi-square Pluto, right from the start Rosie was quick to exploit Pamela's selfless devotion and knew just how to get what she wanted from her elder sister. She could always sweet-talk Pamela into letting her stay up late when their parents were out, and Pamela was an easy touch when she needed some cash or some help with her homework. Yet never once did Pamela feel she was being used or exploited. She enjoyed the warmth of Rosie's company and it gave her genuine pleasure to perform little acts of kindness for her.

As the girls grew up Rosie came to depend increasingly on Pamela's feminine support. She made liberal use of her elder sister's make-up and clothes and took up hours of Pamela's study time pouring out her teenage angst. Whatever Rosie's problem, Pamela was always there with a sympathetic ear, taking the place of their mother whose Saturn contact with Rosie's Moon inhibited a close mother–daughter rapport.

The intimate relationship between the two sisters continued even after both had found husbands, with Pamela still cast in the role of confidante and helper. When Rosie's marriage ran into early difficulties, as usual it was Pamela's shoulder she cried on. And it was Pamela who sprang to Rosie's defence, when it was suggested within the family that Rosie's possessive, manipulative nature may have contributed towards her marriage breakdown.

Naturally it was Pamela who came to the rescue when Rosie needed a child-minder, so she could support herself and her baby after her divorce. With two young children of her own, Pamela considered one more would be little extra trouble and she saw nothing reprehensible in Rosie's failure to offer her any payment. Then there was the babysitting: when Rosie found herself a new boyfriend, Pamela would sleep over at her sister's house a couple of times a week while Rosie was out night-clubbing.

Soon Pamela's whole life began to revolve around Rosie, leaving her little time or energy for her own partner and children, but she felt she had no choice other than to do her very best for her younger sister. She imagined how difficult life must be for a single parent with all the responsibility and worry involved in bringing up a child alone. She felt almost guilty about her own happiness and her own patient, devoted husband and longed to make things a little easier for her sister who had received such a rough deal in life.

Not surprisingly, the patience and devotion of Pamela's long-suffering husband soon began to run dry. As he witnessed his wife's increasing mental and physical exhaustion, he realized she was threatening both her health and their marriage and that unless she gave herself some respite, a further divorce in the family was likely.

It was when she was prescribed tranquillizers for chronic depression that Pamela at last acknowledged she was doing too much and agreed to her husband's ultimatum that Rosie be asked to find a new child-minder. At a loss as to how to find someone as reliable and cheap as her sister, Rosie attempted the usual emotional blackmail to try to change Pamela's mind—her daughter's security would suffer if she were moved, they'd soon be penniless and homeless if she couldn't find someone suitable.

It was a tactic which nearly worked, but not quite. Pamela was beginning to reproach herself for letting Rosie down and may even have relented, had she not received an extraordinary phone-call from her mother, haranguing her for her selfishness and insensitivity to her sister's plight. It seemed that Rosie had conveyed a mangled version of the facts to their mother and had persuaded her to pressurize Pamela into continuing to help her, just for another year until she was financially on her feet.

Her mother's intervention had a catalytic effect on Pamela, bringing to the fore all her suppressed indignation at Rosie's manipulation. After all she had done for her sister without payment or thanks, after the way she had been exploited by her, she felt furiously angry that she should be put in the wrong and have her name blackened within the family. This cruel blow to Pamela's pride opened her eyes to Rosie's lack of concern for her health, her happiness and her reputation. All at once Rosie appeared self-centred and hard, a user who took ruthless advantage of those who loved her and who bore little resemblance to the angelic companion of earlier years.

After Pamela gave up the daily child care for her sister, she continued to babysit on the odd occasion and tried to maintain some sisterly contact. But Rosie clearly bore Pamela a grudge—the accusing look in her eyes conveyed her sense of betrayal and her conspicuous lack of warmth confirmed they were no longer friends.

When Rosie blatantly omitted to invite her sister to her 30th birthday party, Pamela acknowledged their relationship was dead and it was more than two years before they met again to thrash out their differences for the sake of family ties. Pamela misses the intimacy of the past but knows it can never be recaptured. Both women are now different people—or at least they now see each other in a totally different light.

Neptune–Mercury

Perfect intuitive mental rapport or frustrating misunderstandings and deceptions: these are the two extremes of the communication pattern fundamental to relationships featuring Neptune–Mercury contacts.

When Mercury's karmic balance sheet is in credit, she is likely to consider Neptune as an inspiring and empathetic conversation partner, so well attuned to her thoughts and moods that he is aware of what she is about to say before she has even spoken. Neptune's gift to Mercury is his ability to stimulate her imagination, to encourage her to dream a little, to fantasize a little and to give some colour to her strictly logical thinking.

Neptune can often inspire Mercury to express her thoughts more artistically, perhaps in the form of poetry or fiction. Through her relationship with Neptune, Mercury may establish greater contact with her right-sided brainwaves, develop her intuition and get in touch with the creative power of her mind. From Neptune's example Mercury can learn to translate her ideas into reality using the technique of positive visualization.

But when Mercury has challenging karma to face, she may meet in Neptune with her own past maladjusted idealism. Here Neptune may be the kind of person who finds it hard to give creative expression to his vision, may have problems in reconciling his ideals with real life and thus may be prone to misleading himself—and Mercury.

In this case Mercury is likely to find herself a prime victim of Neptune's difficulty in plain speaking, often because she arouses his unconscious memories of a painful sibling or peer relationship from earlier days. In an attempt to redeem the verbal assaults he inflicted or received in the earlier relationship, Neptune now seeks to create perfect harmony with Mercury, a harmony in which no cross word is ever spoken and nothing remotely unpleasant is ever discussed.

However well-meaning, Neptune's evasive approach makes a mockery of the honesty on which any successful relationship must be based. His compulsive—and often unconscious—tendency to withhold from Mercury any information which might prove upsetting frequently leads to serious complications in the relationship, as one untruth leads to another and culminates in a viper's knot of lies and deception. And unless Neptune's integrity is highly developed he may be susceptible to discussing behind Mercury's back the sensitive issues he cannot bring himself to mention face to face. When confronted with the sudden shock of Neptune's verbal deceit and treachery, Mercury's trust in Neptune may be permanently shaken and the relationship irreversibly damaged.

Neptune's lack of honesty is also detrimental to his own well-being. A sense of personal worthlessness, arising from guilt carried over from a previous lifetime, often makes it impossible for Neptune to 'answer back' to Mercury, however great Mercury's verbal provocation. Thus Neptune is frequently incapable of verbally defending himself against Mercury or of giving any assertive feedback, with the result that his anger remains bottled up until some form of escape provides the only release. This poses a serious but often underestimated problem in the relationship, especially when Mercury remains unaware of Neptune's vulnerability to her harsh words or exploits Neptune's passivity. A Neptune child with an insensitive Mercury parent can grow up with an inherent inability to verbalize his hurt and disillusionment and may thus fall into a lifelong role of victim and/or escapist.

Neptune's basic communication problem resides in his unrealistic expectations of himself—and of Mercury. Just as he cannot acknowledge his own need to give voice to negative feelings, he cannot accept Mercury's expression of anger or bitterness. Just as Neptune himself aspires at all times towards a lofty state of mind, he constantly demands an inspired and elevating verbal exchange with Mercury. Inevitably Neptune's longing for euphoric mental contact with Mercury is often frustrated by the banality or coarseness of Mercury's conversation, leading to deep disappointment on Neptune's part.

Neptune's classic reaction to disillusionment is to bury his head in the sand. Unable to fight, he runs away from any situation he finds unacceptable and in a relationship with Mercury will escape by cutting off at the mental level. Neptune–Mercury contacts thus are frequently marred by Neptune's inattention to what Mercury is saying, which can be not only infuriating to Mercury but also wounding to her self-esteem, especially when she is a child. The spaced-out Neptune parent who never gives a clear answer and who constantly dismisses the Mercury child with a preoccupied 'not now dear' is giving the youngster a clear message that she is verbally ineffectual and not worth listening to. No less exasperating is the case of the dreamy Neptune child who seemingly has his head in the clouds and who persistently ignores vital instructions from a long-suffering Mercury parent.

It is not uncommon for Mercury to come to believe that Neptune is actually deaf, since she so often receives an inappropriate answer or none whatsoever from the absent-minded Neptune. In reality Neptune's deafness is rarely clinical but psychological and arises from his tendency to blank out the gross and the mundane. As part of his fantasy perception of Mercury, he hears only what he wishes to hear, projects his own thoughts and ideas onto her and misinterprets her pronouncements. Neptune's resultant misrepresentation of Mercury is commonly labelled as treachery, although in most cases the treachery is unintentional rather than premeditated.

With three planets including Mercury in Virgo, Helen was ill-fitted to fulfil her daughter Michelle's ideal of a gentle romantic motherfigure, the type who is a prolific inventor of fairy-tales and a source of inspiration to a young girl's dreams. Certainly Helen had dutifully supplied a nightly bedtime story, but her unimaginative delivery and punctual adherence to lights-out time frustrated Michelle's insatiable thirst for literary stimulation. Astrologically the problem was symbolized by Michelle's Neptune conjunct Helen's Mercury.

As a stereotyped wife and mother of the post-war era, Helen was a skilled and dedicated housekeeper who was entirely satisfied with the domestic monotony of her life and whose pragmatic values placed small importance on the intellectual emancipation of women. She felt she had little in common with her bookworm daughter, so little in fact that she sometimes doubted she was her own child.

Helen tried her inadequate best to show some appreciation of Michelle's early written work, short stories she composed in every minute of her spare time and which she would bring shyly to her mother for approval. But Michelle's yearning for inspiring feedback was constantly disappointed by her mother's pedantic appraisal of her spelling and grammar and she soon learned to keep her efforts to herself.

Later in life she came to realize how much her confidence in herself as a writer had been shaken by Helen's unintentional put-downs, but she was never able to talk to her mother about her feelings of resentment, either as a child or as an adult.

Despite Helen's lack of sensitivity towards her, Michelle had been keenly in tune with her mother's feelings ever since her parent's divorce when, as an impressionable seven year old, she had listened to her mother sobbing night after night. Although most outsiders would have attested that Helen was as tough as nails, the memory of her mother's vulnerability remained firmly implanted in Michelle's heart. From that time onwards she could never bear to see Helen upset, and it was for this reason that she tended unwittingly to conceal things from her which she believed might cause her pain.

As she grew up, however, Michelle's inability to speak honestly to her mother forged an ever-widening chasm between them. Furthermore, as she became increasingly familiar with the limited range of Helen's conversation—her petty preoccupation with food quality and prices, her nit-picking criticism of others' personal appearance and habits—Michelle found that she had less and less to say to her mother. Helen's small-mindedness bored and disgusted her, she experienced an irresistible urge to yawn in her company, she felt she became zombie-like, perhaps as a means of protecting herself from the soul-destroying trivia of her mother's chatter.

Michelle devoted herself to her schoolwork with the aim of leaving home for college at the earliest opportunity. But her studies were interrupted when she fell in love at the age of 16 with a man who subsequently proved to be married. Unable to face the condemnation of her mother's bourgeois morality, she concealed every trace of the love affair from Helen, inventing excuses for evening outings and the occasional overnight away from home. It was a stormy relationship of 12 months duration which ended in heartbreak for Michelle—heartbreak she was obliged to keep from her mother, who would never have understood what she was going through. Desperate, however, for a shoulder to cry on, she finally confided in a friend who duly passed the story on to Helen.

When she discovered that her teenage daughter had been the mistress of a married man, Helen's merciless castigation of Michelle was prompted not only by shock at her daughter's year-long deception but also by her anger towards her ex-husband's young girlfriend—anger which she now unwittingly transferred onto Michelle.

Despite being labelled by Helen as a whore, Michelle internalized her feelings of betrayal and tried to make her peace. A relationship of sorts continued for the next two years until Michelle finished school and abruptly moved out, leaving behind a brief goodbye note for her astonished mother.

It took Helen some time to recover from Michelle's departure, which only confirmed her opinion of her daughter as devious and unreliable, and she felt once again that she had been stabbed in the back. Nowadays the relationship works much better from a distance, and both women have discovered that they communicate more easily by letter. Michelle, in particular, finds she is freer to express her feelings when she is out of her mother's presence. She realizes now she expected too much of Helen, tries to accept her as she is, but is sad that they will never have the intimate mother–daughter relationship she always hoped for. She feels her mother is no longer part of her life, but she still receives precognitive warning when Helen is unhappy or unwell and her sixth sense always alerts her to an imminent letter or phone-call.

Neptune–Venus

The pure, celibate love associated with this cross-aspect lends itself more readily to platonic friendships and parent–child relationships than to romantic liaisons which require sexual consummation. For the love Neptune offers Venus is specifically non-physical, entailing no personal gratification—it is a selfless, unconditional love capable of sustaining itself under all circumstances, even in the absence of reciprocation.

When Venus is destined to meet with good karma, she can be inspired by Neptune's example to restrain her sensual appetites and refine her cultural tastes. Neptune can help Venus to develop subtler value judgements, to cultivate her artistic interests and gifts and can provide her with a more visionary, intuitive outlook on life.

Every Neptune–Venus contact begins on a note of euphoria with Neptune often driven to the heights of ecstasy by Venus's angelic good looks, charm and style. If Venus is a woman, she is likely to appeal to Neptune's ideal of chaste, unblemished womanhood; if Venus is a man, he will attract Neptune especially on account of his apparent gentleness and sensitivity. In either case Neptune's eulogistic praise and devotion have little to do with sexual desire, a fact Venus should be aware of from the start to avoid subsequent frustration. Indeed, when Neptune plays the male role, he can often develop a quasi-religious obsession with a Venus woman, worshipping her as a madonna-like figure whose virtue must not be deflowered.

Most of the problems which arise in Neptune–Venus relationships derive from Neptune's over-idealized moral and aesthetic perception of Venus and his unreasonable disillusionment when his false beliefs are exposed. Sooner or later Venus will seem less physically pleasing, less innocent, less cultured and a good deal more crass than she appeared initially to Neptune. And when this happens Venus may be shocked by the depths of Neptune's contempt for her in the wake of his raving idolatry. In the meantime Neptune's ill-conceived and ill-expressed idealism is likely to have spun a web of guile and self-deception of which Venus is invariably the hapless victim.

Neptune's virginal fantasy of Venus may compel him to try to protect her from the crude realities of life at all costs and, if necessary, to resort to lies and subterfuge. Matters relating to Neptune's finances and social life are often considered by Neptune as too potentially disturbing to Venus to be openly divulged— perhaps due to Neptune's recall of Venus's suffering on these counts in past lives or perhaps due to his sense of personal guilt towards Venus. But whatever the karmic background, the reality of Venus's relationship with Neptune is that she must often learn to live with obsessive secrecy on his part, particularly where money and relationships are concerned. She must somehow come to terms with Neptune's chronic lack of honesty, which at best amounts to vagueness and at worst to downright deceit and perfidy.

In effect Neptune is no more feckless or unfaithful than any other planetary role; it is simply that his guile, his scheming and his bare-faced denials make his sins appear more dastardly and more deeply wounding to Venus. The sense of loss associated with a lover's faithlessness is hard enough to bear, but where long-term deceit and betrayal are also involved the situation can be devastating. Equally, the partner who is clearly hopeless with money is a pain, but far worse is the one who claims to be flush with funds whilst surreptitiously courting financial ruin.

Always, for Venus, it is the fact of not knowing about Neptune's indiscretions, of being kept in the dark until the point of no return, which is so traumatic. For rarely does Neptune's behaviour reveal anything of his secret world.

To all appearances Neptune is the devoted partner, the paragon of conjugal virtue, who seems dedicated to bringing happiness into the life of the beloved, no matter what the personal cost. Indeed, it is not uncommon for Neptune to make a complete doormat of himself, driven by the very same urge to protect his loved one which also leads him to deceive her.

Taken to extremes, Neptune's yearning to serve the object of his worship can produce the hen-pecked husband, the downtrodden wife or the parent-dominated child, especially when Venus falls in an exploitative sign and is prepared to take advantage of Neptune's subservience. This too is an unhealthy development which can ultimately rebound upon Venus, when Neptune finally tires of his masochistic game and makes a subtle exit.

Whether it is Neptune who withdraws from the relationship or Venus herself, invariably it is Venus who has the hardest task in overcoming a deep sense of abandonment and treachery. It is difficult for Venus to come to terms with the sordid depths to which Neptune can stoop when things go wrong, compared with his heady romanticism at the start of the relationship. Yet it is precisely Neptune's urge to perpetuate his initial sense of elation that gives rise to his self-delusions and their disastrous consequences, and understanding this fact can help Venus to summon up the unconditional love required to forgive Neptune's shortcomings.

Venus can do much to minimize her problems with Neptune by persistently demanding open discussion of every issue which arises, and especially those concerned with money or relationships with other people. Neptune should be reminded by Venus not to project his own value judgements upon her and not to presuppose that she would be upset by the revelation of the truth. Encouraging Neptune to give creative expression to his idealistic yearnings in artistic pursuits is another tactic whereby Venus can help to contain his more dangerous fantasies.

The Neptune–Venus cross-aspect is capable of producing an entire gamut of emotions, ranging from the bitter desolation of unrequited or betrayed love to the spiritual ecstasy of the perfect union. At its highest level, Neptune symbolizes platonic love in its true sense of love for the individual which inspires contemplation of the universal. But in order to reach such heights the two people must also have their feet firmly planted on the ground. They must be willing to accept the crude realities of their earthly relationship, whilst still holding onto their dream.

Des was a country boy, feeling lonely and bewildered in the metropolis where he had just arrived after the recent death of his parents. Joan was an urbanite, totally at home with the fast pace of city life and delighted to welcome her innocent boyfriend into the bosom of her large, close-knit family.

Homosexual by instinct although not by practice, Des had not previously had a steady girlfriend, but with the approach of his Saturn return was thinking about settling down and finding himself a wife/housekeeper. Having always shied away from blatantly sexual women, he felt comfortable with Joan's demure, well-scrubbed good looks, characteristic of her Sun–Moon Virgo conjunction.

Because it suited Des to perceive Joan as a sexually undemanding companion, his Neptune exactly trine to her Venus in Scorpio remained blind to her latent passion, focusing instead on her strength of character, her loyalty and her unswerving moral and emotional support. Deeply grateful to Joan for the affection she offered him at a time when he most needed it, he came to believe that she would make a good wife and that with her he might at last start a family of his own which he had always wanted but which until now had appeared an unattainable dream.

It was some four years after their marriage before Joan presented Des with a son and heir. It had been a difficult pregnancy and an even more distressing labour, which provided Des with the perfect excuse to break off their sexual relations and return to his former celibate status. Love-making had never featured strongly on their marriage agenda, but now Des beat a final retreat to his own bed in an apparent act of self-sacrifice, claiming that abstinence was the only sure means of sparing Joan the pain of a further pregnancy.

Joan's reaction to the enforced termination of her sex-life was ambivalent: her Sun–Moon conjunction in Virgo was quite happy to exist without a lover, but her Venus in Scorpio demanded nothing less than total emotional and physical union and felt furiously frustrated. Although superficially she accepted Des's judgement, it reinforced her inherent insecurity and as the years passed she became increasingly possessive and jealous. Unaware of Des's basic disinterest in the female sex, she convinced herself that his physical indifference to her derived from his involvement with another woman—a misconception that was not remedied by her husband's persistent unpunctuality, vagueness and inability to account for time.

To Des, Joan's bitter accusations of his infidelity were inexplicable—with Venus in Aquarius, possessiveness was alien to his own nature and he had never suspected its existence in Joan. It was also deeply disappointing, destroying his fantasy image of Joan as an emotionally mature companion, and dashing his hopes that their relationship would remain free of sexual complications. Indeed, what he had originally interpreted as Joan's puritanical aversion to sex now presented itself as a neurotic obsession with sex, for she seemed to talk of little else. As his disillusionment with his marriage grew, thoughts of divorce began to enter Des's head and may even have materialized if Joan had not suddenly collapsed with an attack of paralysis.

The shocking diagnosis of multiple sclerosis led to a complete change of outlook on Des's part, banishing all ideas of separation and arousing feelings of compassion for Joan he had never before experienced. He threw himself unstintingly into an exhausting routine of nursing care, house care and child care, spurred on by self-reproach that his inadequacy as a husband may somehow have contributed to his wife's illness. His sense of guilt had its roots in his childhood loss of his younger sister whom he felt he had treated unkindly and whose death from leukaemia had weighed heavily on him. Now once again he blamed himself and feared that Joan too might die, unless he were somehow able to redeem his ill-use of women.

One of Des's tactics to minimize Joan's suffering was his insistence that she should not be informed of the true nature of her condition, believing that with her emotional instability she would be unable to cope with the prognosis and would fare better in ignorance. He took upon himself the burden of keeping the dark secret concealed from his wife, which further added to his stress and drove him to seek increasing solace in alcohol.

Joan took full advantage of the slight disability she was experiencing in the early stage of her illness to double her emotional demands on Des, perhaps in an attempt to pay him back for wrecking her love-life. Despite his attentiveness, Joan never appeared satisfied, her accusations continued unabated and it seemed she would not be content until she had made a complete prisoner of her husband.

Des found it hard to reconcile his disgust at Joan's possessive, manipulative nature with his genuine love and concern for her and his longing to protect her from suffering. He could see no way out of his dilemma and he was eventually diagnosed as suffering from terminal cancer.

Suddenly the situation was reversed, and to everyone's surprise Joan stepped easily and willingly from the role of patient to nurse, caring tenderly for her husband to the very end, apparently having laid to rest all her old recriminations. Indeed, as a widow she always spoke in the fondest terms of her late husband and claimed that her marriage had been blissfully happy.

Neptune–Mars

Such is the mystical fascination that Mars holds for Neptune it is not uncommon for Neptune to be utterly besotted by Mars's drive, courage and sexual charisma. Indeed, Neptune will often perceive Mars as a hero figure, personifying the loftiest of masculine virtues, regardless of whether Mars is a man or a woman and regardless of Mars's actual accomplishments. At the highest level Neptune's idolization of Mars's animus can form part of a karmic service Neptune has chosen to render to Mars: by visualizing Mars as a white knight Neptune helps to ennoble Mars's expression of power and male energy.

Neptune's enraptured response is usually quite beguiling to Mars: indeed it is difficult for Mars not to be seduced by the atmosphere of euphoric excitement created by Neptune when they are together. Neptune–Mars contacts are often characterized by a state of mutual entrancement in which both people feel themselves to be permanently on a high.

Sometimes Mars's instincts may warn her correctly that Neptune's manic adoration is just too good to be true, that there is little real substance to his protestations of love. In romantic relationships Mars may become suspicious of Neptune's failure to give physical expression to his emotions and may wisely question the authenticity of Neptune's passion. For the truth is that there is rarely much sexual interest on Neptune's part, and although a sensation-seeking Neptune may occasionally entice Mars into debauchery, in general his feelings for Mars are romantic rather than erotic. If Mars is hoping for a predominantly lustful relationship, Neptune's strictly spiritual interest can be both frustrating and disappointing.

The main problem for Mars in this association resides in Neptune's inability to reconcile his lofty vision of Mars with the real person—his unwillingness to accept the 'dark' side of Mars, linked perhaps to an inability to accept his own 'darkness'. When Neptune's idealism is inadequately grounded, he may attempt to shut out from his consciousness all aggressive feelings towards Mars in the pretence that such feelings do not exist. Here Neptune may be motivated by a sense of guilt and remorse about past-life conflicts with Mars—or with someone of whom he is reminded on an unconscious level by Mars.

Regardless of Neptune's self-deception, the odds dictate that sooner or later he will be unable to maintain his fantasy and will be coerced into a clearer perception of Mars—perhaps by a transit of Saturn, Uranus or Pluto. Then what Neptune formerly considered as assertiveness on the part of Mars he will now see as belligerence, what formerly appeared to be incisiveness will now appear as impulsiveness and what he once took as boldness he will now judge as foolhardiness. Neptune may also now begin to reject the sexual advances of Mars, which he once glamorized as an expression of romantic fervour but which he now disdains as gross bestiality.

Neptune's puritanical revulsion at Mars's coarseness stems from his basic fear of acknowledging his own animal desires and his anxiety to avoid all situations likely to trigger those desires. In an attempt to keep the relationship totally pure and spiritual, Neptune will flee from all passionate confrontations with Mars: rows are anathema to Neptune and must be evaded by tactics ranging from feigned deafness to feigned or actual sickness. A favourite excuse of Neptune's is that he is too weak or sick to argue—which usually successfully disempowers Mars but also frustrates Mars's need to clear the air.

This emotional cowardice on the part of Neptune can be especially damaging to a Mars child, whose will is subtly undermined by an inadequate Neptune parent, sometimes a semi-invalid, but at any rate without the physical resources to handle the child. Often such a child is made to feel guilty about expressing negative feelings and may have problems in self-assertion later in life. A sense of guilt may also be instilled into a Mars child by a Neptune parent who is unable to accept his own sexuality, and who causes the child to grow up feeling ashamed of its physical drives.

Neptune's fear of confrontation with Mars frequently manifests in lies and subterfuge as a means of eluding the aggressive response he imagines may ensue. This projection by Neptune of the anger he himself might experience in Mars's place is something both people should be aware of to prevent the classic pattern of deceit which can occur with this cross-aspect. If Neptune can only experiment with being completely honest with Mars, he is often pleasantly surprised at the outcome.

Neptune's dishonesty basically arises from his excessive expectations of himself. In the desire always to appear in a good light he feels compelled to conceal from Mars anything which might reflect badly upon himself. Neptune's aspirations towards sainthood can also manifest in his martyred submission to Mars where, instead of evading Mars's physical aggression, he chooses to become its victim. It is interesting that in neither case is Neptune willing to face Mars square on. Especially when Mars is of the type likely to exploit Neptune's weakness, Neptune may willingly subject himself to considerable physical and sometimes sexual abuse by Mars, often as a result of guilt carried over from past incarnations.

Neptune's persistent refusal to take up the gauntlet can be severely detrimental to the relationship in terms of the frustration or over-indulgence of Mars's will, and the energy imbalance this creates. Sooner or later the relationship is likely to crack under the strain, usually as a result of Neptune's withdrawal when finally he can take no more.

But a Neptune–Mars contact need by no means always be difficult. When the two people involved are aware of the likely pitfalls and maintain scrupulous honesty and realism, they can function exceptionally well together as a self-inspired team. Whilst Neptune can inject a little imagination into Mars's creative exploits, Mars can infuse Neptune with the energy to actualize his dreams and fantasies. And just as Neptune can help to refine and spiritualize Mars's raw aggression, Mars can encourage Neptune to give vent to his anger without fear or guilt. Above all, the relationship can form a vehicle whereby the two people forgive themselves, and one another, for all past and present acts of aggression in the expression of unconditional love.

With Mars in Aries, Nick had all the qualities required of a successful salesman: assertive, resilient and single-minded, he was rarely defeated in any objective he had set his mind on. He tended to adopt the same go-getting approach in his relationships, having always had an eye for a pretty girl, although he had no intention of leaving his wife—that is until he met Samantha.

Sam, who worked as a secretary for one of his clients, was totally different from the self-assured, flirtatious women to whom he was normally attracted. She was gentle, shy and noticeably lacking in confidence, she enjoyed talking about spiritual topics, of which he knew nothing, and she had an unfulfilled ambition to become a nurse. She seemed to him to be the sweetest, kindest and most fascinating woman he had ever met, reflected by his Mars in opposition to her Neptune. She also appeared to be the most unattainable, and he was genuinely surprised when she accepted his offer of a drink and even more so when, several dates later, she agreed when he asked her to sleep with him.

Sam too was surprised at the strength of her feelings for this man who shared none of her own outlook on life but for whom she felt an overpowering desire. She was turned on by Nick's directness, his blatant virility and his undisguised impatience to get her into bed, and she felt convinced that making love with him would be the ultimate sexual experience of her life.

Perhaps her judgement had been clouded by the large quantities of alcohol they habitually consumed on their dates, for when the big night finally arrived her expectations far exceeded the reality. But despite her disappointment in the sexual side of their relationship, she still felt attracted to Nick on some level and continued to date him and to sleep with him.

Her interest in the relationship now resided in the satisfaction she gained from helping Nick to discover his aptitude for spiritual healing, which revealed itself when he visited the psychic circle of which she was a member. Nick in turn encouraged Sam to actualize her dream of becoming a nurse by building up her self-esteem, infusing her with some of his own ample drive and finally persuading her to apply for training.

Sam was indebted to Nick for all the support she had received from him and she cared for him deeply as a friend, but not as a lover. In fact she was contemplating how best to break off their affair when Nick announced unexpectedly that he had left his family and wished to move in with her. Stricken by self-reproach that she had separated him from his wife and children, Sam felt unable to dispel Nick's false hopes and agreed that he should temporarily share her flat, since he had nowhere else to stay.

The relationship ticked over for a few months, but faking an orgasm was becoming increasingly tedious for Sam and she felt she couldn't keep up the pretence much longer. Finally, when she found herself strongly attracted to a man on her training course, she knew the time had come to level with Nick and to ask him to leave. But such was her sensitivity to his vulnerability, such was her fear of hurting his volatile feelings, she could never quite find the words to tell him their romance was over. She could do no more than hint that she was no longer sure how she felt about him, and she began dating the new man without Nick's knowledge.

When the inevitable occurred and Nick discovered that Sam was cheating on him, he immediately challenged her with his usual fiery directness. But he was puzzled and frustrated by Sam's refusal to explain herself and her tendency to burst into tears or lock herself in the bedroom in response to his questions. Sam, for her part, still felt too afraid to admit to Nick that their romance was over, and his anger only increased her sense of guilt and confusion. She couldn't bear to think that they might end up as enemies and cherished the vain hope that the relationship might continue on a platonic basis.

Even when Nick's rage finally erupted into violence, she still failed to face up to facts, reproaching herself instead of him and believing she thoroughly deserved her bruises. It was left to Nick to end their relationship in the knowledge that he could no longer cope with the frustration of being kept dangling on a string. He loved Sam far too much to risk hurting her again, and he knew this is precisely what would happen if they remained together much longer.

Nick spent a painful period of rehabilitation adjusting to existence without Sam. She had been such an important part of his life for so long, but in retrospect he felt he had never really known her and that they had each had conflicting expectations of the relationship. She had often told him she thought they were soulmates, but her frigidity and deviousness made it difficult for him to believe her.

Nick was helped over his heartache by the comfort he received from the healing circle, which Sam quit discreetly shortly after the break-up. His ability to empathize with others was undoubtedly quickened by his own suffering and he now spends much of his spare time helping the sick in mind and body, working as an accredited and highly respected spiritual healer.

THE KARMIC
CROSS-ASPECTS OF PLUTO

Pluto–Ascendant

Pluto cross-aspects are well known for arousing more passion, intrigue and pain than any other planetary contacts. These relationships invariably entail some kind of fatal attraction where the two people are trapped by their powerful feelings for each other, often against their will and their better judgement. Frequently they are motivated by factors which they do not understand and over which they have little control, since their basic interaction takes place at the level of their unconscious.

People involved in Pluto cross-aspects tend to relate to each other profoundly and sometimes with disturbing intensity. Pluto in particular is likely to experience an activation of his psychic energy field, which attracts the other person by magnetic force and which can be used, depending upon Pluto's degree of enlightenment, either for healing purposes or for self-gain.

Since, in a Pluto–Ascendant cross-aspect, it is the physical appearance of the Ascendant player which forms the basis of the attraction, the mutual impact is usually immediate and compelling. The Ascendant player often feels—and acts—as if she were hypnotized, hopelessly unable to resist Pluto's charismatic power, rendered inert like prey transfixed by its predator. Even from the start the Ascendant player is likely to be heavily emotionally dependent on Pluto and may experience an irrational fear of being parted from him. And as the relationship deepens, this fear may develop into a belief that she could not continue to exist without Pluto, frequently due to the influence of a previous incarnation in which her physical survival was indeed dependent upon Pluto.

Pluto invariably displays an uncanny clarity of insight into the Ascendant player—a seeming ability to penetrate the depths of her soul, which can be both fascinating and unnerving to the Ascendant player. When Pluto has attained the appropriate level of spiritual development he may use this perceptiveness to provide the Ascendant player with a helpful analysis of her hang-ups and the best means of overcoming them. A positive Pluto never forces change upon the Ascendant player but merely casts light on those of her behaviour patterns which are outworn and in need of release. Pluto the healer never attempts to mould the Ascendant player into the person he would like her to become but allows her to develop according to her own needs whilst supplying emotional support and sustenance.

When Pluto has chosen to render a karmic service to the Ascendant player, the relationship can provide the framework for tremendous two-way growth. In other cases, however, it can form the scenario for a mutually destructive power struggle, in which the two people may inflict unbelievable suffering on each other because of their inability to let go. Everything depends upon Pluto's own state of spiritual well-being. If Pluto has done little work on his own psyche and cannot consciously identify with his fears, projecting these instead onto others, he is likely to react defensively, manipulatively and cruelly towards the Ascendant individual without ever realizing that he is doing so.

When Pluto is the vehicle of the Ascendant player's hard karma, the physical characteristics of the Ascendant player are likely to waken Pluto's subconscious memories of a past trauma which seriously undermined his security. Sometimes Pluto is reminded by the Ascendant player of a specific individual who threatened his survival or at other times of an unacknowledged and menacing aspect of himself.

Indeed, Pluto's fascination with the Ascendant player is closely bound up with his recognition of personal traits which he has long been too fearful to express due to a sense of vulnerability. Fundamentally Pluto is attracted to himself in his perception of the Ascendant player and will tend to behave towards her much as he behaves towards himself. Thus to the extent to which Pluto attempts to repress his own 'forbidden' traits, he will seek to control these in the Ascendant player.

The tactics employed by Pluto to maintain a position of power over the Ascendant player can range from overt bullying to subtle emotional blackmail, depending upon his own chart position and the sign of the Ascendant player. In general, however, he will ruthlessly exploit his depth of insight into the Ascendant player to play on her weaknesses, undermine her self-confidence and reinforce her emotional dependency on him.

The power games beloved of Pluto can never take place without the Ascendant player's passive participation, and despite her protestations of ill treatment she frequently invites, or at least accepts, Pluto's domination. In many cases the Ascendant player has become accustomed to subservience to Pluto in past-life working or family relationships and now is unable to break out of the mould. In a challenging Pluto–Ascendant contact both people are often locked into their respective roles of master and victim, and there can be no prospect of achieving a more balanced relationship until each acknowledges and ceases the collusion.

Where the two people are romantically involved with each other the power struggle can take on a more desperate and potentially violent nature. The sexual attraction in a Pluto–Ascendant cross-aspect is often inescapable and obsessive, and the sexual rapport between the two people is exceptionally profound since they tend to give of themselves completely. For this reason parting is proportionately more painful, the urge to hang on more compulsive and the ending of a love affair more difficult to come to terms with.

The theme of domination and submission is also of crucial significance in parent–child relationships in which the Pluto player, whether child or parent, will exploit his natural emotional hold over the Ascendant player in order to indulge his own will. Not uncommonly a Pluto child can mercilessly bully an Ascendant parent who feels confused and enraged by her ineffectiveness in resisting the child's demands, unaware that she is trapped in a past-life relationship pattern in which the parent–child roles were reversed.

Normally, however, it is an Ascendant child who is most vulnerable to the pushiness of a Pluto parent, simply because it is the adult who possesses the greater physical clout. And unless the Pluto parent is in touch with the reality of his manipulative tendencies and his own motivation, he risks suppressing the child's individuality or will and of driving her prematurely away in search of freedom.

Indeed, a frequent outcome of Pluto–Ascendant cross-aspects is that the Ascendant player is forced by unbearable pressure to break away emotionally and/or physically from Pluto, involving considerable anguish and heartache on both sides. For Pluto the challenge is to release the object of his obsession and to cope with the inevitable upsurgence of resentment without permanent damage. The Ascendant player must also learn to let go and must struggle with her fear that survival without Pluto will be impossible—although usually she discovers that it is not, thus breaking a karmic bondage which may have spanned many lifetimes.

For both people involved in this kind of relationship mutual release is the inescapable goal, each being compelled at some point to overcome their attachment to the other, if only through the inevitability of death. Generally it rests in the hands of Pluto as to whether this process will be accomplished with more or less difficulty, depending upon his willingness to trust, relinquish control and go with the flow. Only when Pluto lets go of his unconscious insecurities is he likely to accomplish his own self-healing. And only when he lets go of his need to control the Ascendant player can he exert any healing influence upon her in turn.

At the highest level Pluto–Ascendant cross-aspects can provide a loving, supportive framework for mutual transformation and regeneration and for release from stagnating karmic ties. It is a question of how each individual aligns and utilizes his or her will as to what extent this potential can be fulfilled.

It was a stormy, windswept evening in mid-November when Harriet first set eyes on Karl. He cut a dramatic figure with his long blonde hair and full-length black leather coat, appearing as if from nowhere to help repair her car when she broke down on a country lane. They exchanged phone numbers by way of courtesy, but during the days that followed she found herself repeatedly thinking of him and hoping against hope that he might contact her. When he finally rang she felt ecstatic but was unable to explain to herself or her curious girlfriends exactly what she found so attractive about him.

By all appearances he was grossly unsuitable—15 years her junior and still a penniless and carefree student, here to study English before starting professional training in Germany. She, on the other hand, had heavy financial and emotional commitments, working long hours as a teacher to raise her sons single-handed. But his Pluto in Leo conjunct her Ascendant defied all reason, compelling her to invite him to move in with her just a couple of months after their first meeting.

Initially their sex-life was predictably exciting and steamy. After five years of celibacy Harriet was captivated by her handsome young boyfriend's passionate love-making, even though he was a little rough at times and there was rarely any foreplay. Karl too couldn't get enough of Harriet at first—he was spellbound by her extroversion, self-assurance and her Leo ability to turn heads wherever she went. He had always been attracted to sophisticated older women of her type but most were too contemptuous of his impoverished immaturity for him to strike up any kind of relationship with them.

Harriet, however, was different. Beneath the outer veneer she had a vulnerable, naïve side and she continuously turned to him for practical help and advice, as on their auspicious first meeting. In one sense he saw her as a little girl but at the same time she reminded him of his mother with whom he had had a close relationship until her death when he was just 10. He was particularly drawn towards Harriet's solid maternal qualities and initially admired her dedication to her sons, although before long this became the source of a powerful feeling of jealousy and resentment of the boys. The fact that there was only some 10 years difference between their respective ages intensified the sense of rivalry and elicited some childish temper tantrums on Karl's part when he felt insecure.

It was not long before Karl also began to take out his frustration on Harriet herself. It started of course in bed, where he delighted in punishing her by beginning to make love to her and then switching off at the last minute. But the main scenario for Karl's game-playing was at parties and social gatherings where he would exploit the power of his natal Mercury–Pluto square to run verbal rings around Harriet and make her appear intellectually inferior. He also took pleasure in humiliating her by publicly revealing doubts she had confided to him about her teaching ability and career standing.

At the root of Karl's discontent lay a desperate craving for the recognition he had failed to receive as a child from his stepmother, and which he had mistakenly hoped he might obtain from Harriet. It wasn't just the boys who got in the way: Harriet's own flamboyant personality overshadowed his restrained Scorpio Ascendant which found it so difficult to be open and spontaneous, especially with his language problem, and reinforced his basic sense of inadequacy. When Harriet showed off, commanding all the attention, he found it impossible to contain the spiteful, caustic remarks that spewed out from deep inside him and which were so devastatingly effective in deflating her ego.

Gradually the scenes and the outbursts drove away most of Harriet's old friends and she found herself increasingly alone with her sullen companion. Even her sons spent more and more time out of the house, and they finally begged their mother to kick Karl out because his boorish behaviour was making their life unbearable. Certainly Harriet was aware that she needed to do something about Karl, but she was at a loss as to how to handle him and make him behave more reasonably.

The fact was that with her own Venus in Scorpio square Pluto, Harriet was inherently incapable of supplying Karl with the unreserved, unmeasured love which he desired so badly and which was the only thing which might have transformed the relationship. Having been badly hurt by men in the past, she found it impossible to open up to his emotional needs and to identify with his insecurities. Instead she was able to see the situation only from her own angle, rigidly locked into her own doubts and fears.

It was Karl's deteriorating behaviour towards her sons which gradually drove Harriet to stand up to him more and to begin to distance herself from him emotionally. Karl's reaction to Harriet's sudden coolness was likewise that of withdrawal. He now stopped making love to her completely, stayed in bed all day and spent most nights out clubbing, squandering the pocket money he regularly extorted from her.

Harriet surprised herself by not crying when Karl finally packed his bags and walked out one Sunday morning, announcing that he had found a new girlfriend who really loved him. She just felt an overwhelming relief that the ordeal was over and that at last he had made the break, because she knew she herself would always have felt powerless to do so.

Pluto–Sun

When Pluto forms a close cross-aspect with the Sun, the Sun is likely to be compulsively drawn towards Pluto by a deep sense of empathy. The Sun may feel that Pluto understands her ambitions like no one else and that she will receive dedicated emotional support from him in the pursuance of her goals. Soon she may even come to believe that Pluto's back-up is essential to her success and that without him she can achieve nothing.

The magnetic pull is almost as strong on Pluto's part, inasmuch as he is confronted in the Sun with a long-lost facet of his own creative drive, an experience which can be both fascinating and threatening. The Sun has the effect of triggering Pluto's unconscious memories of his past creative self-expression, and where these memories are traumatic Pluto may need to defend himself by using his psychic power to destroy their source, i.e. the Sun.

When Pluto's unconscious recall is less menacing, he will find it easier to use his psychic energy to regenerate and heal the Sun and in turn will be open to personal growth through his relationship with her. Through her example the uninhibited Sun can help Pluto to overcome his own insecurities, learn to trust and regain his confidence in the area of life symbolized by the Sun's sign position.

In a harmonious relationship Pluto can serve as a mirror to the Sun, gently unmasking her overtly egocentric traits, such as excessive pride, vanity and ostentation, so as to improve her effectiveness and well-being. He can also utilize his depth of perception to point out where the Sun's career or self-expression has entered a rut and would benefit from a change of direction.

But when Pluto is operating from a position of unconscious fear he may exploit his insight into the Sun's vulnerable self-identity by undermining her confidence and manipulating her lifestyle with the motive of controlling her for his own purposes.

Pluto's need to overpower the Sun arises sometimes because the Sun reminds him of a father-figure who once threatened his security and from whom he now feels compelled to defend himself. In most cases, however, the Sun symbolizes a repressed aspect of Pluto's own creativity, which was rewarded in the past by punishment or loss and which Pluto now struggles to control both in himself and in others.

When Pluto feels the need to attack the Sun's ego, he will set about this task by planting and nurturing seeds of self-doubt which in time may multiply into a major crisis of self-image for the Sun. Pluto is a master in the art of playing on the Sun's craving for recognition, pushing her beyond her capabilities and souring her satisfaction with her achievements. With Pluto's subtle encouragement the Sun can come to question the worth of everything she has worked for and eventually may come to consider herself an abject failure.

Once Pluto has successfully subverted the Sun's chosen form of creativity, he occupies a strong position in which to force her into a different area of self-expression with which he feels more comfortable and less threatened. Usually this is an area with which the Sun feels far from comfortable but which she attempts to follow in subservience to Pluto. Sun children with Pluto parents are particularly likely to suffer in this way by having their natural talents frustrated and criticized and being forced into a mould which they do not fit.

So subtle is Pluto's control, the Sun is often unable to recognize that she is being manipulated until her self-esteem has been completely destroyed. The Sun's difficulty in acknowledging her powerlessness can also derive from past-life experiences where her self-expression was subject to Pluto's authority, either in a working situation or in a parent–child relationship. Perhaps the Sun's very survival was dependent at that time on her compliance with Pluto's will, a compliance she senses she must maintain in this incarnation in order to guard her life.

It can be especially hard for a Sun female with a Pluto partner to assert her independence due to women's traditional projection of their self-expressive drive onto their menfolk. When a woman is lacking in clearly defined personal ambitions and has an inadequately developed self-image, she may remain indefinitely an unquestioning victim of Pluto's domination, unable to break free until Pluto moves out of her life by death or by his own volition.

Little change can occur in the hard karma the Sun faces in her relationship with Pluto until she learns to reclaim the power she has given away, releases her emotional dependence on Pluto and reassumes her rightful position at the centre of her universe. In so doing she enforces a healthier relationship balance where both people are obliged to let go of their mutual dependence and take personal responsibility for their insecurities. If it is to survive and flourish, a Pluto–Sun relationship must be prepared to break free of the shackles of karmic bondage and base itself on genuine trust, love and respect.

Linda had always been drawn to macho men. Her first boyfriend was a rally driver and her second, who became her husband, was a dynamic young broker who rapidly made a name for himself in the City. She herself had plenty of drive as a youngster but her father had brought her up to believe that girls stay at home to bring up the children and she had fulfilled his expectations. By the time of her divorce at the age of 35 she had never worked outside the home and was far from realizing her childhood ambition to open a fashion boutique.

A generous divorce settlement had, in fact, supplied her with the potential capital to turn her dream into reality. But her problem lay with Ricky, her strong-willed 10-year-old son, whose Pluto in opposition to her Sun in Aries had always made heavy demands on her freedom. With his irascible, antisocial temperament he was not the type of child to be entrusted to a minder and he threw such tantrums if left with Linda's mother, that she had refused to care for her grandson until he calmed down.

Linda convinced herself that Ricky was bound to become more manageable as he grew older and that she would be able to launch the shop when he was a teenager. But with adolescence his rebelliousness only increased, and during the course of his four-teenth year she was summoned three times to the school because of his involvement in fights. She felt incapable of making any plans for her career while Ricky was going through such a disturbed phase, and she hoped that the security of her continual company might save him from delinquency.

She was also held back by Ricky's obvious disapproval of her desire for a career and his adeptness at convincing her that she couldn't cope with the competitive world of retailing. But despite Linda's self-sacrifice things grew worse rather than better, and when Ricky was finally suspended from school for threatening to strike a master Linda felt fearful for his future.

She had always nurtured great ambitions for her son, hoping that he would go to university as she herself would have liked, then on perhaps to the Foreign Office or some such Establishment post. But with his uncontrollable temper and obvious hatred of authority Ricky was clearly going to find it difficult to settle into any conventional form of employment.

It seemed Linda could do nothing to control her son. With her petite frame she was physically outmatched by his strongly-built physique and deep powerful voice, and her attempts to reprimand him were quickly shouted down. She'd tried all the usual forms of punishment but he just walked out of the house in defiance, daring her to try to stop him. She decided that more contact with his father might bring about some improvement in his attitude but after the first unwilling visit he announced that his stepmother was a shrew and he had no intention of going again.

The truth was that Ricky longed for his father's company but had ambivalent feelings about the divorce, secretly fearing that his own bad behaviour might have driven his father away. Deep inside he was worried that his mother too might eventually abandon him, and although he knew that his rebelliousness was alienating her, he felt driven by demons and unable to change.

Ricky's emotional insecurity reached crisis point when Linda began dating a new man-friend and at last seemed to be building a life of her own. Ricky tried his usual verbal persuasion, running down the new man and warning Linda of the problems the affair was likely to cause her. When this tactic didn't work, he resorted to scaring her, staying out at night, refusing to reveal his whereabouts and coming home drunk. Stricken by panic, Linda threatened to send him to live permanently with his stepmother, although in reality she couldn't bear the thought of losing him and at this stage had no intention of implementing the threat.

Her announcement was intended to make a forceful impact but she was totally unprepared when Ricky immediately lashed out at her with his fists, unaware of his own muscle power, dislodging his mother's front tooth and colouring her eye black and blue. It was something both of them agreed could never happen again, as Ricky wept with remorse and Linda convinced herself that the attack had been a momentary aberration. But after Ricky struck her the third time, Linda knew that for both their sakes she must take drastic action.

It was the hardest decision of Linda's life: when Ricky moved in with her ex-husband and his new wife she felt she had deserted and betrayed her son and feared she could not live with her guilty conscience or the loneliness of the empty house. But within a couple of months her anxieties were dispelled by a cheerful letter from Ricky, who had quickly settled down in his new home and had already made a number of new friends. His dramatic change in temperament was due largely to his reunion with his father, something he had yearned for since the divorce but had never been able to articulate.

For Linda too, life is nowhere near as black as she dreaded it would be. At long last she has opened her fashion boutique where she sells her own designs run up by a small team of co-workers. Her relationship with her new boyfriend is deepening and for the first time in her life she is doing precisely as she pleases.

Pluto–Moon

Pluto–Moon contacts are unique among cross-chart aspects in terms of their capacity to bring about deep emotional regeneration and healing. When Pluto has chosen to render karmic service to the Moon, he can provide her with unswerving emotional support and can help her to shake off negative response patterns. In Pluto the Moon has access to a personal psychoanalyst who is always keenly perceptive of her emotional state, regardless of how well it may be disguised.

In addition Pluto can help the Moon to reassess her attitudes towards her family, especially her relationships with her children or parents where these are the result of past conditioning and are in need of transformation. At the karmic level the function of Pluto is to supply the Moon with the necessary psychic energy to seek out and release the source of her emotional hang-ups, whether these originated in childhood or in past incarnations. But this is only possible where Pluto is in touch with his own emotional pain and insecurity and is himself open to self-healing and change.

Right from the start the Moon's emotional security is almost entirely invested in Pluto, so it is hardly surprising that she experiences a tremendous emotional dependence on him. And because the Moon is highly sensitive and vulnerable to every change of mood on the part of Pluto, her happiness, stability and peace of mind are closely bound up with him.

Clearly Pluto wields tremendous power in this cross-aspect, especially in the case of intimate family or sexual relationships, a power which Pluto may be tempted to abuse by subjecting the Moon to subtle emotional blackmail. For example, there is the temptation for Pluto to use his unfailing insight into the Moon's psyche to play on and manipulate her feelings so as to bend her to his own will. And especially when the Moon is a child, she may suffer untold emotional damage by having her security constantly threatened by Pluto in this way. Thus unless Pluto's morals are of the highest calibre, his emotional hold over the Moon can be detrimental to her rather than beneficial and can reinforce her vulnerabilities rather than dispel them.

Pluto's emotional manipulation of the Moon is generally due to a sense of threat from her instinctive emotional responses, since these represent a repressed aspect of his own feeling nature, forced into retreat as a result of childhood or past-life trauma. At the same time the Moon may remind Pluto of a mother-figure from the past who undermined his emotional security. But in either case Pluto's defences are triggered and he will seek to ensure that he retains the emotional upper hand.

In order to do this Pluto will attempt to penetrate into the deepest recesses of the Moon's heart, although he himself is normally unwilling to share much of his own feelings. Slowly but surely Pluto will prod away at the Moon's inner self, until he has uncovered every secret and the Moon begins to feel that she no longer has any emotional privacy. Pluto can be the type of partner who opens his spouse's letters in case she is keeping anything from him, or the type of mother who pries into her child's diary, incapable of accepting the child's entitlement to a separate emotional identity.

Not uncommonly the Moon may come to feel that she has been subjected to psychic rape and must seek some form of escape from Pluto. Here it is vital that the Moon is resolute in demanding more emotional space from Pluto and is not held back by her karmic dependence upon him and her fears for her survival without his support. This can be especially important for a Moon child, who risks lifelong emotional domination by a Pluto parent unless she asserts her independence early on.

Pluto will sometimes react to the Moon's emotional desertion by going to extraordinary lengths of revenge, perhaps finally banishing the Moon from his life as the ultimate gesture of power. In other cases he may come to terms more gracefully with the Moon's karmic evolution, actively encouraging her to move beyond her dependence on him and to take personal responsibility for her emotional security.

Once Pluto relinquishes his need for emotional control over the Moon, he can draw personal benefit from greater openness to the Moon's feeling nature and the possibility of learning from her as an emotional role model. Now Pluto in turn can receive emotional support from the Moon, allowing him to experiment with giving uninhibited expression to the 'dangerous' feelings he has repressed for so long.

Trust is an essential factor in this process of mutual transformation, trust on the part of both players that letting go need not lead
to pain. Fundamentally the acquisition of this trust may be
dependent on a strong spiritual faith and the conviction that when
we choose to take positive action in a spirit of love and respect,
ultimately the outcome can only be joyful.

When Giles met Sally she was just 19, the only child of a broken
home and suffering from all the usual emotional instability. Having
been abandoned by her father at the age of 9 and alternately
ignored and bullied by her Scorpio mother, she was desperately
searching for someone who would love her unreservedly and
whom she could love unreservedly in return. Giles too was
searching for the 'real thing', although at the age of 48, with one
failed marriage and a string of unhappy affairs behind him, his
hopes of finding the perfect woman were slowly beginning to fade.

But with her Moon in Libra exactly trine to his Pluto, Sally made
an instant impact on Giles's heart and only five minutes after their
first meeting he felt that he was talking to an old friend. Just a
couple of dates later he was convinced that he had at long last
found his princess, his soul-mate, the dream girl he had been
waiting for all his life.

For several weeks he floated on a high but was finally obliged to
confess to himself that with the huge age gap the relationship was
probably untenable. Although he had never before felt such a deep
and immediate emotional rapport with any woman, he dared not
hope that one so young and so beautiful as Sally could feel
anything more than a passing infatuation for him. And in a valiant
attempt to do the 'right thing' he accepted a six-month contract
abroad in the expectation that Sally would soon forget him.

But Giles had not reckoned with the strength of Sally's feelings
for him and her perseverance in convincing him of her love. At
long last she had found in Giles all the tenderness, support and
undemanding affection she had lost when her father disappeared
from her life and which she had never been able to rediscover in
her relationships with boys of her own age. Now she had a
boyfriend who cared for her as a whole person rather than just a
sex object, and she had no intention of giving up without a fight,
regardless of their age difference. She took the first flight available
to join him and when she fell into his arms, tearful and dishevelled
after her long, exhausting journey, they both knew their future lay
together, whatever challenges destiny had in store.

In fact, the main challenge in their relationship centred around Sally's emotional hang-ups. She felt a good deal of anger towards her domineering mother, which her Libran cowardice had never allowed her to express and which she concealed beneath a cloak of feigned indifference and politeness. But with Giles's help she began to see how her passive acceptance of her mother's bullying had actually encouraged this behaviour and slowly she acquired the self-confidence to stand up to her more. With unfailing patience Giles lent his shoulder for Sally to cry on, urging her to pour out all her bottled-up parental resentment and gradually rebuilding her self-esteem. When finally Sally announced to her disapproving mother that she would be marrying Giles with or without her blessing, she was astonished by her immediate capitulation and her unexpected attendance at the wedding.

But it was more difficult for Giles to make much headway with Sally's basic distrust of men, an insecurity which had originated with the departure of her father and which she now inevitably projected onto Giles. Perhaps also it was because of the initial threat of losing Giles that Sally suffered a neurotic anxiety that he might suddenly disappear from her life, her greatest and most irrational fear being that Giles would not return if he left her for a few moments in a restaurant or club. Sometimes she could scarcely bear to let Giles out of her sight and despite his constant protestations of devotion and love, her nagging doubts persisted and detracted from her rightful happiness.

Strangely Sally's fears usually focused on the possibility that Giles might desert her and rarely that he might die, despite her awareness that she would probably be widowed at a young age. For this reason it was an appalling shock when she awoke one morning, after almost five years of marriage, to discover that Giles had suffered a fatal heart attack during the night.

After Giles's death Sally felt more alone than ever before, believing herself to be incapable of continuing life without him. She longed to follow him to 'the other side' and contemplated suicide on several occasions, but each time was pulled back from the brink by a band of loyal friends. A series of readings with a talented medium helped to convince her of Giles's spiritual survival and gave her the will to carry on courageously, as she knew he would have urged her to do.

Years later she came to realize that it was through the joy and the pain of her short years with Giles that she had accomplished most of her growing up. It was as a result of Giles that she finally became a woman, that she gained the emotional maturity to take on a testing relationship with a man closer to her own age, someone who was also prone to insecurity and whom she was able to offer a little understanding.

Pluto–Mercury

Every Pluto relationship is based on a charismatic attraction of some kind; in the case of Pluto–Mercury cross-aspects, this attraction plays out at the level of the intellect. It can often appear to Mercury that Pluto has achieved an exceptionally high level of mental power or that he is in possession of some secret knowledge which holds a fatal fascination for her. In other cases Mercury is stunned by Pluto's ability to read her mind, to know what she is thinking even before she does herself, and she may believe him to possess extrasensory perception.

At the highest level Pluto can utilize his telepathic link with Mercury to reflect back her innermost thoughts in the manner of a psychic mirror. He can encourage Mercury towards greater intellectual integrity, gently questioning her statements and encouraging her to reassess her opinions and beliefs where these are ill-defined or outmoded. Ideally he will be able to pick out the flaws in Mercury's reasoning and clarify her thought processes without ever offending her mental pride.

Indeed, so powerful is the mental support and stimulation offered by Pluto, he can soon become indispensable to Mercury, who may eventually feel incapable of thinking for herself or solving any problem without Pluto's assistance. This is an unhealthy dependence, often the legacy of a past-life relationship between the two individuals, where Mercury was subject to Pluto's intellectual authority, for example a pupil–teacher relationship. And it is a dependence which must be overcome by Mercury if she wishes to sever her karmic bondage to Pluto and reclaim her mental autonomy.

Mercury may well be pushed into ending this dependence by Pluto's tendency to selfishly exploit his power over her. Indeed when Mercury has challenging karma to face in her relationship with Pluto, she may be so browbeaten and brainwashed by Pluto's attempts to control her that she is finally compelled to seek escape.

Pluto's overt tactics in proving his intellectual supremacy consist of conversation domination and ruthless exposure of Mercury's errors in logic and speech. More subtly he can attempt to wield thought control over Mercury by keeping a constant check on the contents of her mind and playing on her mental anxieties. 'What are you thinking about?' is the constant demand that Mercury can come to resent, as Pluto relentlessly proceeds to suck her mentally dry.

It often seems that Pluto will not be satisfied until he has gained total knowledge and control of Mercury's thought patterns, an obsession which is usually triggered by his unconscious fear of Mercury and an urge to defend himself against her. Sometimes Mercury's ideas remind Pluto of an intellectual stance once held by himself but for which he suffered punishment and has ever since sought to repress. In other cases Mercury may remind Pluto of a hated authoritarian figure from his past by whom he was punished for thinking along 'forbidden' lines. In either case Mercury's mind represents a threat to Pluto's security and he must prevent her at all costs from gaining power over him.

Whatever Pluto's motives, the end result for Mercury can be a sense of intellectual inferiority as her ideas are repeatedly shot down as worthless, and a sense of verbal frustration as her attempts at communication are repeatedly interrupted. The impressionable Mercury child, growing up with an insensitive Pluto parent, teacher or older sibling, is especially at risk from this kind of mental abuse; equally, however, the compulsively argumentative Pluto child who always has all the answers can harass his unfortunate Mercury parent to the point of despair.

If Pluto is to spare Mercury the humiliation of such mental oppression, he must be prepared to look carefully at the source of his mental inflexibility and verbal intimidation—not easy if Pluto is still a child. Not until Pluto is consciously aware of his need to wield power over Mercury can he successfully relinquish his hold and establish a more open and trusting mental rapport with her. Not until Pluto has lowered his intellectual defences can he offer to—and receive from—Mercury the kind of mental regeneration which is possible with this cross-aspect.

When this relationship is working well, Mercury and Pluto can make perfect co-counsellors, each able to supply the other with honest feedback and a level of support and trust which encourages the verbalization of doubts and fears. The two individuals can also stimulate one another to probe more deeply into the unknown and to take the kind of intellectual risks which sometimes result in quantum leaps in knowledge; in particular, they can work well together in any kind of research, especially that relating to science or the occult.

But the success of any Pluto–Mercury partnership is fundamentally dependent on the correct balance of intellectual power between the two individuals and their long-term efforts in maintaining that balance.

Paula was the kind of girl who apparently had it all: good looks, keen intelligence and a rich, indulgent father who paid for everything, including her sports car. At the age of 20 she was idling through the second year of an uninspiring science degree course, diverting herself in the company of countless yuppie boyfriends, all with the same mainstream scientific training as herself, all destined to embark upon a life of uneventful prosperity.

She met Pierre just before the summer exams, when she visited him for a Tarot reading in the company of a group of fellow students desirous of discovering their prospects of success. It was all a huge joke to Paula, who had no belief whatsoever in the occult and considered fortune-telling of all kinds to be fraudulent or self-deluded. She arrived for the consultation in a spirit of contempt with the expectation that her scepticism would be validated. She departed in a state of emotional shock, shaken to the core by the accuracy of Pierre's insights and not least by the intensity of his exquisite blue eyes, which seemed to pierce her very soul, leaving her with a sense of psychic nakedness.

Her first reaction was that of downright anger that she had been victimized by her friends, whom she assumed had supplied Pierre with her personal details to amuse themselves at her expense. What other possible explanation could there be for the Tarot reader's extraordinary knowledge of her pet likes and dislikes, her family members and most of all her intense relationship with her father? Incensed by the blatant invasion of her privacy, she commanded Pierre to confess to the trickery, or to prove the impossible by providing indisputable proof of his clairvoyance.

A natural psychic who used Tarot and astrology as a focus for his intuition, Pierre had devoted the last 10 years of his life to helping the sick, the bereaved and the troubled at heart in return for small donations. He had little time or need to prove himself to non-believers, but there was something about Paula's intelligent outspokenness which aroused his interest and compelled him to take up her challenge.

He noticed immediately that she herself was an undeveloped psychic, denying her gift as so many people do and forcing herself into an area of study that took no account of her sensitivity. Pierre found himself hoping that she might one day become his pupil and invited her to dinner to propound the principles of clairvoyance.

Aware that he would need to address the subject in the scientific terminology with which Paula was familiar, Pierre decided to commence the evening with a highly effective practical demonstration. By an effort of will, he succeeded in fusing the lights as evidence of the unlimited power of the human mind, and then launched into a detailed explanation of the electromagnetic forces responsible for this phenomenon. By the end of the evening Paula was totally fixated by Pierre, a man she had first taken as a simple-minded fortune-teller, but whose intellect clearly outshone that of any of her college boyfriends.

Six months later Paula had dropped out of her degree course, sold her sports car and was living in frugal simplicity in Pierre's downtown apartment—much to the dismay of her doting father.

A self-made businessman from a close-knit Roman Catholic family, Paula's father viewed poverty as a symptom of failure and believed the occult to be akin to devil worship. Fearful for his daughter's material and spiritual well-being, in the first instance he used religious pressure to attempt to prise her from her mentor's grasp. When this failed he resorted to old-fashioned financial blackmail, threatening to disinherit her if she refused to end her relationship with Pierre.

But much as she loved and needed her father, Paula was irretrievably hooked on her brilliant and unorthodox boyfriend. He had opened her eyes to an aspect of science of which she had no previous knowledge but which she found to be of compelling fascination. He had unveiled a previously unexplored aspect of her personality, the intuitive side of her which responded to the intangible rather than the tangible, to feelings rather than to logic.

She had always been aware that her sharp mind was capable of analysing any factual problem but had previously distrusted her ability to function at the emotional level. Yet now, with Pierre's guidance, she discovered an outstanding talent for psychometry—that simply by holding a small object she could accurately describe the owner's state of mind and the main recent and forthcoming events in their life.

Paula is now co-writing a book on parascientific research with Pierre and has embarked on a study of psychology. Despite a three-year period as lovers, their relationship is now platonic: after the initial fascination petered out, Paula began to feel oppressed by Pierre's intellectual dominance and needed to reassert her independence. Her Mercury in Scorpio gave her a natural resistance to sharing her thoughts, and with Pierre's telepathic ability she often felt she hadn't got a private thought in her head, which was rather unnerving.

These days Pierre and Paula are the proverbial good friends, working happily and successfully together, but careful to give each other plenty of space, as befits the square cross-aspect between his Pluto and her Mercury.

Pluto–Venus

Pluto–Venus contacts are associated with the most powerful emotional, and where appropriate, sexual attractions found in any cross-aspect. Pluto's sexual–psychic energy field is invariably stimulated by Venus's physical appearance, social graces or artistic talents. It depends on Pluto's level of spiritual evolution and Venus's karmic account as to whether Pluto will use this energy to possess and control Venus or to promote her regeneration and healing.

Venus cannot be other than profoundly affected by Pluto, often finding it impossible to resist his compelling gaze. When Venus has suffered domination by Pluto during previous lifetimes she may now feel threatened by him and may experience the urge to escape before she is completely consumed. But when the karmic bondage between the two people is strong this may be difficult for Venus. Pluto–Venus relationships are thus often based on a fatal attraction where Venus, against her better judgement, is sucked into a potentially self-destructive relationship from which she is unable to free herself.

Where the two individuals' past-life associations have been harmonious, Venus may feel more comfortable with Pluto's intensity, instinctively sensing his loyalty, dependability and devotion. Indeed, when Pluto is prepared to give unconditionally, this cross-aspect can symbolize the deepest of love bonds based on mutual trust and surrender.

Pluto invariably exhibits a marked insight into Venus's psyche. When he is functioning at the highest level he will use this sensitivity to respond promptly and fully to Venus's emotional and sexual needs. Pluto may also be capable of analysing and healing Venus's social and financial problems and of positively transforming her artistic expression and personal presentation.

But where Venus is destined to experience challenging karma in her relationship with Pluto, Pluto may attempt to manipulate Venus by exploiting her emotional vulnerability and is especially prone to use sex and/or money as a means of asserting his control. In other cases Pluto may attempt to prove his power over Venus by remoulding her appearance or by influencing her style of artistic self-expression in accordance with his own ideas.

Pluto's compulsive domination of Venus is motivated by his fear of Venus's anima. In Venus he is confronted with an aspect of his own feminine sexual and creative energy, which he is unable to express openly—usually on account of earlier trauma—and which he is unwilling to acknowledge. Simultaneously attracted and repelled by the self-image he perceives in Venus, Pluto must often resort to strong-arm tactics in order to protect himself. Venus may also remind Pluto of a female figure dating from his childhood or from a past life, a female who threatened or destroyed his security and from whom he must now defend himself.

By virtue of their very intensity, Pluto–Venus cross-aspects can give rise to marked extremes of love and hate which manifest predominantly in sexual relationships. These are the all-consuming love affairs, capable of inspiring heights of ecstasy which can just as easily turn into despair and hatred. Often present is an element of obsession, where one person becomes fixated with the other and unable to release him or her from their thoughts. Jealousy is often a major problem, whether there is cause for distrust or not, and in the event of actual infidelity the desire for revenge can be overpowering, especially on the part of Pluto.

Jealousy is also likely to arise in parent–child relationships of this type, where either individual's fear of losing the other can inspire spiteful, manipulative behaviour. Where Pluto plays the role of parent, his dominating tendencies can seriously inhibit the development of a Venus child's aesthetic, artistic and social values and will be resented to a greater or lesser extent by the child depending upon its age and Venus's sign placing. A crisis usually occurs during the Venus child's adolescence, when her burgeoning independence can cause her to baulk at Pluto's attempts to control her dress, her friends and her cultural tastes.

Equally, however, a possessive Pluto child can wield considerable emotional power over a malleable Venus parent, manipulating and undermining her relationships—frequently her relationship with the other parent—and imposing incessant financial demands which Venus feels unable to refuse.

The most effective means of transforming a Pluto–Venus relationship is for Pluto to recognize and overcome his fear-induced need to subject Venus to his control. Once this is accomplished, Venus's love and empathy offer Pluto the chance to test out in a safe environment the modes of creativity he has long repressed in himself and to which he is so uncomfortably attracted in her.

With Venus's encouragement Pluto can experiment with new artistic activities, with a new approach to money, or perhaps just with enhancing his personal appearance. The primary challenge for Pluto is to trust and to free himself from his insecurities; only then can he begin to learn from Venus and discover the healing resources with which he can help Venus in turn to overcome her own insecurities.

Where Pluto is unwilling to change, Venus can break the deadlock by psychologically releasing herself from Pluto through visualization. This simple technique is often sufficient to change an oppressive relationship into one which is healthier and more balanced, since Pluto's domination of Venus can exist only with Venus's co-operation and cannot cease until she ends her collusion. It is a good idea for anyone whose Venus is strongly aspected by another person's Pluto to practise psychically releasing the Pluto individual whilst the relationship is still sound. This eases the inevitable pain of parting commonly experienced by Venus when Pluto eventually disappears from her life.

Patrick was a suave and successful businessman in his late thirties who had used his Mars in Capricorn to build up a business specializing in the production of electronic components, but whose creative Venus in Leo conjunct Pluto was largely unexploited. To fill the void he financially supported upcoming young artists, sponsoring local exhibitions to seek out undiscovered talent. It was at one such exhibition that he made the acquaintance of Monica, who was showing her paintings for the first time and who instantly impressed him by the passion of her work.

With Venus in Scorpio, Monica was somewhat cautious of rapid involvement with men, but for some inexplicable reason she was compulsively attracted to Patrick from the first moment she caught sight of the back of his head. He had an electrifying effect on her both emotionally and physically and she confided to a friend, not entirely in jest, that he was the only man she had met who could give her an orgasm just by looking into her eyes.

She had little difficulty in seducing him or in capturing his heart, and before long he was proposing to her on bended knee, declaring he would die if she refused him. Patrick had nothing to fear on that score, however, for Monica was hopelessly infatuated with him, basking in that special blend of paternal and erotic love that only an older man can offer. At Patrick's request she gladly gave up her part-time job to devote herself entirely to her art, ensconced in the vast attic studio of Patrick's home which he had converted for her at great expense.

It was little more than a couple of months before the challenging nature of his Pluto square her Venus began to manifest. Since he was paying all the bills, Patrick felt entitled to some say in the kind of paintings Monica was producing and persuaded her to change from abstracts to portrait work, which he believed would find a larger market and bring in more money.

He seemed obsessed with the commercial potential of Monica's art, using his business expertise to find sales outlets and taking complete control of her finances. From her earnings Monica was allocated only a small personal allowance—Patrick paid for almost everything she needed. On the whole she did not question her financial accountability to Patrick, since she respected his business expertise and was happy to leave her career affairs to him. What she did loath, however, was having to ask her husband's permission every time she needed new underwear or a new pair of shoes.

To Patrick it seemed quite natural that he should control his wife's finances—it was part of his macho philosophy. He also saw nothing wrong in choosing and paying for Monica's clothes: he loved to flaunt her curvacious figure in the expensive, tight-fitting and low-cut dresses which he bought for her as presents, and which he expected her to wear whenever they went out together.

Although she found his taste vulgar and out of keeping with her style, she tried at first to comply with his wishes in the manner of a dutiful wife. Later, however, she began to feel angry with herself for betraying her self-identity and allowing herself to be dominated. Finally she refused to wear anything she hadn't chosen herself, which Patrick took as a personal insult and a sign of rejection. The clothes issue fast developed into a major point of contention between the couple and the focus of the insidious power struggle which lay at the heart of their problems.

A major turning-point in the relationship occurred when Patrick ordered Monica to take off a dress she had bought for a dance they were to attend together, complaining that it made her look fat and frumpish. She burst into tears, stung by the harshness of his words: it was the first time he had ever criticized her looks and she was surprised how much it hurt and just how much she needed his approval.

Suddenly acknowledging the extent of her emotional dependence on Patrick and the marked absence of other relationships in her life, Monica began to contact some old girlfriends with a view to reviving her social life and boosting her morale. But Patrick's boorish rudeness soon drove them away again and Monica was once more alone.

It was during a Uranus transit that she finally decided she'd had enough. Although her portraits were fetching a good price, she wasn't doing the kind of work she wanted to do and she had no control whatsoever over her income. She had lost most of her self-respect and most of her friends, and she was possessed of a terrifying sensation that the life was being squeezed slowly out of her.

Patrick opposed the divorce and went out of his way to make things as difficult as possible for Monica, stubbornly refusing to revoke the five-year contract she had signed appointing him as her manager. Monica is currently involved in legal negotiations to attempt to free herself from her contractual obligations to Patrick. Despite the fact that they are now living apart, she still feels haunted by Patrick and his desire to continue to control her financially. Releasing herself from Patrick's economic hold over her is actually proving a good deal more difficult for Monica than breaking away from his emotional domination.

Pluto–Mars

The attainment of any kind of harmonious interplay between these two planets is inherently problematic, since neither is concerned with harmony but rather with confrontation. The best possible outcome of this cross-aspect is that the two individuals may help one another towards a regeneration of their physical drive and psychic energy, but before this can happen each must be prepared to probe into and release their long-standing subconscious anger towards the other.

There is usually a very strong bodily awareness between Pluto and Mars, which in some cases amounts to sexual attraction or in others consists simply of mutual respect for the other person's physical strength and charisma. This powerful physical response can also generate a sense of anxiety, causing each person to feel threatened by the other's sexual and psychic energy field and consequently to adopt an aggressive or defensive stance.

Fiery Mars usually has little difficulty in acknowledging and expressing her antipathy, but Pluto's fears operate more at the unconscious level and thus may be slower to manifest. Pluto's fears will often derive from a half-forgotten past-life association with Mars in which his security was injured as a result of Mars's physical aggression or in which, in the worst of cases, he may have lost his life at Mars's hands.

Where there has been no past-life relationship between the two people, Pluto's fears may arise simply from Mars's resemblance to a physically menacing individual from his childhood. More commonly, however, it is Pluto's self-association with Mars's animus which arouses his alarm, half-awakening an unconscious masculine quality of Pluto's which he fears to express and keeps deeply hidden.

Whatever his motivation, Pluto's suspiciousness of Mars compels him to attempt to outwit Mars on every possible occasion and to pre-empt a possible attack by establishing psychological and often physical or sexual control of Mars.

But of all the inner planets Mars is the most resistant to Pluto's domination, the least hint of conflict rousing her mettle and activating her will. Mars will instinctively defend herself from Pluto in accordance with her sign placing, thus revealing the very mode of assertiveness of which Pluto is so afraid and compelling him to adopt ever more sinister tactics in an effort to reclaim control. The ultimate winner will be dependent upon each planet's natal strength and the karmic account between the two individuals. Certainly Pluto is a much dirtier fighter than Mars, willing to wait indefinitely for victory, but he can easily be put out of action by the sheer speed and ferocity of Mars's attack.

In defeat Mars finds it a good deal easier than Pluto to accept that she has lost the battle. For Mars the conflict with Pluto exists only at the physical level or at the level of the personality and can be released relatively easily through meeting new challenges. But because Pluto functions predominantly at the psychic level, his feelings inevitably run deeper and his bitterness and need for revenge may continue indefinitely, poisoning his future relationship with Mars and often with others also.

In the final outcome everything depends upon Pluto's willingness to come to terms with his ongoing rage towards Mars and to discharge his negative feelings towards her; it is this which governs the extent to which the healing potential of this cross-aspect can manifest. Only when Pluto relinquishes the need for revenge and develops some degree of trust can he begin to function as a vehicle of spiritual energy, thus bringing about his own regeneration and helping Mars in turn to transmute her aggression.

Here Pluto can utilize his clear perception of Mars's energy patterns to pinpoint the strengths and weaknesses of her self-assertion and goal pursuit. At the same time he can maximize his receptiveness to Mars as a role model of courageous and incisive self-expression, who can help him to find a safe outlet for that side of his animus which he has previously feared to acknowledge.

Pluto–Mars is the cross-aspect especially connected with sexual violence, which can occur when Pluto feels hopelessly threatened by Mars's sexuality and cannot resist the urge to bring Mars to submission. In romantic relationships the Pluto partner, generally male, may resort to brutality in order to compensate for a sense of sexual inadequacy. In parent–child relationships also, an inadequate Pluto parent may be tempted to affirm his power over a Mars child by sexual or physical abuse.

In whatever context they are enacted, Pluto–Mars cross-aspects can be associated with actual bodily as well as emotional pain, since it is Mars's function to draw forth into physical form the psychological conflicts arising from Pluto's subconscious. Through Mars, Pluto is confronted with a concrete image of his own unexpressed aggression and through Mars he can come to acknowledge, discharge and transmute that aggression into light.

Where Pluto is resistant to self-awareness and self-change, it may be necessary for Mars to extricate herself from Pluto's domination to avoid a mutually detrimental, deadlock situation. Here Mars is challenged to use the positive side of her nature to respond assertively but non-violently to Pluto's bullying and to detach herself from Pluto's karmic hold—not always easy for Mars when her association with Pluto spans many lifetimes.

In those cases in which Mars finds herself trapped against her better judgement in a compulsive, painful relationship with Pluto, it may be necessary for Mars to acknowledge her own involvement in this situation before she can successfully break free.

When Mars is faced with the destructive expression of energy in her relationship with Pluto, she is generally meeting with her own past misuse of physical power and/or condonation of violence. Thus it is fundamentally only by rejecting rather than colluding with Pluto's violence that Mars can sever her past-life bondage to Pluto and can simultaneously clear her own karmic account.

Although Tina described her first meeting with Barry as having been struck by a bolt of lightning, it took her over a year to arouse his interest sufficiently for him to ask her for a date. With her Mars square to his Pluto, Tina experienced a powerful and immediate sexual desire for Barry, coupled with a faint sense of fear. His strongly built, muscular frame towered almost a foot above her, causing her to feel simultaneously excited and physically intimidated.

It was precisely Barry's strong macho persona which appealed to Tina's natal Mars in Scorpio, the masculine side of herself which she had always projected onto the 'dangerous' types of men to whom she was habitually attracted—men like Barry with a reputation for philandering and violence, men who were both fearless and powerful.

Having struggled long and hard to develop her femininity to compete unsuccessfully with a sensationally pretty younger sister, Tina had always rejected her own masculine drive despite its obvious strength. She remained sadly unaware of the stirling qualities of courage and fortitude which others always noticed in her and for which she was picked out in her nursing work to deal with patients in the worst pain and shock.

Like Barry, Tina had a childhood background of domestic hostility and tension, but whereas her middle-class parents had never openly expressed their enmity towards each other, Barry's dominating, hot-tempered mother had often hospitalized his father as a result of their violent clashes.

Well used to keeping her feelings concealed, Tina was hopeful that with an emotional extrovert like Barry as a partner she would at last be able to be herself, but the first time she lost control and burst into tears he slapped her hard round the face and dismissed her as hysterical. From that moment on she lost all her trust in

Barry, together with most of her respect for him, but it took more than a decade for her finally to break away from the powerful hold he wielded over her.

For Tina the next 10 years were filled with the pain and shame of repeated assaults, resulting in almost continual bumps, bruises and scratches. She soon became adept at concealing her scars with long sleeves and dark glasses and at skilfully circumnavigating the probing questions of suspicious friends. Curiously it never occurred to her even to consider leaving Barry. Her strict religious upbringing had convinced her that marriage was for life—in her eyes she had made her bed and would have to lie in it despite her growing revulsion at Barry's crude sexual demands and her total lack of sexual satisfaction.

It wasn't that she felt no fury towards Barry. She often fantasized about plunging a sharp blade deep into his heart and was careful to hide the kitchen knives from herself in case she should succumb to the terrible temptation. But in reality she was incapable of expressing her anger in any way, partly because of her emotional conditioning but also because she knew it would only lead to more physical punishment from Barry. Aware that whatever she said or did, he would always get the better of her, she became accustomed to spending increasing time on her own and sank deeper and deeper into depression.

Then two developments occurred in her life which brought about a sudden change of outlook. Attending a hospital party alone one evening against habit, she met a charming doctor who made her feel feminine for the first time in years and with whom she had a short but passionate affair. The resultant boost to her self-confidence made her look at her life with Barry in a fresh light and question her resignation to her unhappy marriage. Around the same time she began to study astrology, obtaining some insight into the workings of her personality and her behaviour patterns in relation to men.

Slowly she began to become more assertive, perhaps overly so in order to compensate for her years of subservience. Once considered amiable and easy-going, she now gained a reputation as a tyrant among the young student nurses in her charge, unwittingly venting her resentment towards Barry on anyone over whom she exerted power. More importantly, she refused to cover up for Barry's violence any longer and threatened to sue him for assault if he abused her again.

And although she still didn't divorce him, it occurred to her that it would be convenient if Barry could find somebody new. Perhaps

it was with this in mind that she engaged a beautiful Scandinavian
au-pair, who promptly fell hopelessly in love with Barry and he
with her.

It was not so much finding them in bed together that pushed her
into the final decision to walk out of the marriage. It was more her
sense of utter destitution when, a short while later, she was
confined to bed for two weeks with severe 'flu during which time
Barry never even brought her a cup of tea.

As soon as she recovered she packed her bags, but not without
first laying down the terms of her financial settlement and
discharging her bitter feelings towards Barry. Suddenly, with the
prospect of release, all her repressed fury surged up inside her, her
fury at the years of open flirtations, the degrading insults, the total
lack of tenderness and appreciation and not least the physical
injuries. For the first and only time in their relationship she tore
her nails into Barry's face, leaving him with a disfiguring memento
of her revenge.

The heavens were thundering on the day she left, but she
danced through the rain, warmed by an unfamiliar sense of self-
gratification and conscious that in retrieving her self-respect she
had taken the most important step of her life.

Tina has now progressed to a senior nursing position, having
undergone retraining in the psychiatric sector. She is still proud of
and happy with her new-found independence, and no one who
meets the confident, assertive woman that she is today can believe
that she subjected herself to so many years of degradation.

THE BALLAD OF JOHN AND YOKO

It was perhaps the most fascinating romantic partnership of the century: two eccentric artists, both talented in their own genre, both having suffered emotional trauma at various phases of their lives, drawn together by a fateful attraction for one another which ended John's marriage to his first wife Cynthia and changed his life irrevocably.

It was also a liaison which to many appeared inexplicable. Unable to perceive the subtle links which drew the two lovers together, the fans found it hard to see what Beatle John, the rich and famous sex symbol, found so seductive in the little Japanese woman, nearly 10 years his senior. 'A passing infatuation' was the general consensus, a relationship which could not possibly last.

But last it did, and the absorbing question presents itself as to what made the partnership so special. What planetary influences governed this outrageous love affair between two apparently unsuited individuals? What karmic factors lay behind the well-publicized fights and partings, but above all the enduring mutual devotion which kept them together despite all the odds?

To an astrologer, the deeply committed but at times unstable relationship between John Lennon and Yoko Ono bears the unmistakable hallmarks of Pluto and Uranus, and indeed those planets feature prominently not only in the cross-aspects between the two charts but also in Yoko's own natal chart.

Having Uranus in her seventh house almost exactly square to her natal Pluto, Yoko is a compulsive rebel, a woman of indomitable will who makes a formidable impression on many who come into contact with her. Although quietly spoken and unassuming in manner, she possesses a powerful charisma and undoubtedly played the dominant role in her two former marriages, both of which she ended of her own volition.

With John's Ascendant and Sun forming hard aspects to Yoko's natal Uranus–Pluto square, he was highly receptive to her special brand of bohemian charm. Never before had he met a woman who radiated, at one and the same time, Yoko's unusual combination of eccentricity, vulnerability and strength of character, symbolizing the dichotomy of his natal Moon in Aquarius opposition Pluto. Perhaps John sensed that Yoko was the perfect embodiment of his anima, and that through her he would become complete in a way that had never been possible in his former relationships with women.

Whatever John's unconscious motivation, soon after his first meeting with Yoko, when at her bidding he hammered an imaginary nail into a wall in payment of an imaginary five shillings, he fell under the oriental artist's spell with all the drama of a classic Uranus–Pluto attraction. Suddenly John felt like a lovesick teenager again, unable to stop thinking about this extraordinary woman, who constantly excited his mind and whom he couldn't bear to let out of his sight.

Unlike his marriage to Cynthia in which by his own admission he had often been unfaithful, from now on John was to become a one-woman man. His life henceforth was to revolve around Yoko and everything else was to become secondary to his relationship with her. John's former attitude to women had been to treat them simply as housekeepers or whores, never as buddies or soul-mates, but with Yoko it was all to be different.

The effects of Yoko's Pluto on John's Sun in Libra manifested not only in his willing dedication to her but also in the seeming control that Yoko began to exercise over his close relationships with others. Gradually John started to cut himself off from almost everyone who had been important to him in the past—his son Julian by his marriage to Cynthia, his half-sisters in Liverpool, his old pals at Apple and finally even the other three Beatles.

If Yoko was indeed behind John's sudden withdrawal from those who loved him, we might ask what she saw of her own unconscious in John that made her so afraid of his close associations with others. Despite her Libran Ascendant, unmistakable in her serene smile and tranquil disposition, Yoko found it difficult to make close

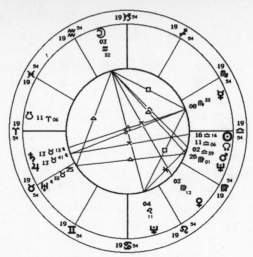

John Lennon

Oct 9 1940   5:30 pm GMT
53N25   2W55
Oct 9 1940   17:30:00 GMT
Tropical Equal True Mode

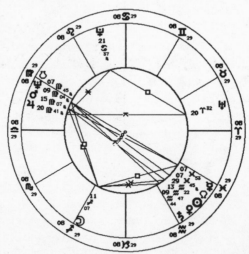

Yoko Ono

Feb 18 1933   11:30 am GMT Japan
35N40   139E45
Feb 18 1933   11:30:00 GMT
Tropical Equal True Mode

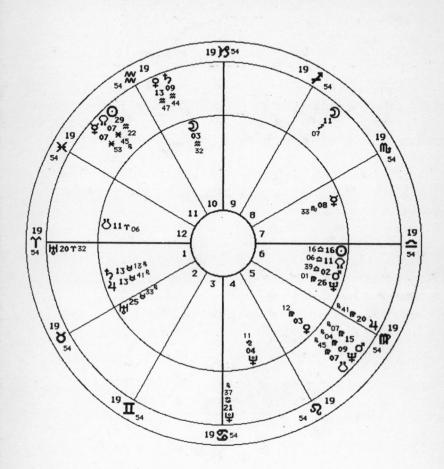

John Lennon

Oct 9 1940   5:30 pm GMT
53N25   2W55
Oct 9 1940   17:30:00 GMT
Tropical Equal True Mode

Yoko Ono

Natal Chart
Feb 18 1933
11:30:00 GMT

friends, being basically detached and independent. In this respect she differed completely from John who had always had at least one bosom pal right from childhood. It may be that Yoko felt threatened by John's easy expression of this undeveloped side of her own personality. Or any possessiveness on her part may have been triggered by karmic memories of having lost John in past lives.

Even closer than the contact between Yoko's Pluto and John's Sun was the tight Pluto–Ascendant cross-square between them, symbolizing Yoko's attraction to—and need to defend herself from—John's Aries persona. John's irascible temperament, fierce outspokenness and readiness to lash out with his fists when under pressure were tough-guy qualities, which Yoko had not met with in any of her former men and which clearly struck a chord in her own animus.

Certainly on the one hand her attraction to John seems to have been largely based on her admiration of his macho personality— her Uranus conjunct his Ascendant was undoubtedly exhilarated by his impulsiveness and belligerence. Yet the question arises as to whether in setting herself up as head of the household, taking control of their financial and business affairs and allowing John to assume a domestic role, she did not unwittingly set out to 'emasculate' him.

At best Yoko's Pluto–Uranus may have diverted John's open aggression into a more productive form of self-assertion, such as the political campaigning they embarked upon together. In becoming an activist for peace John was tethering his desire for confrontation to his need for harmony and at last giving effective voice to the Aries–Libra polarity of his birth chart, a duality which had led to so many bitter fights and reconciliations with friends prior to his relationship with Yoko.

But by no means was John Lennon entirely under Yoko's thumb. Firstly his own Pluto widely opposed her Venus in Aquarius and widely trined her Moon in Sagittarius, suggesting that he in turn exercised some hold over her detached and independent emotional nature. And secondly the inherent rebelliousness of his natal Venus–Uranus square firmly precluded any possibility that he could ever simply disintegrate into a hen-pecked husband. Furthermore, given that Uranus was almost equally as significant as Pluto in the cross-aspects between the couple, their deep emotional union was balanced by an unsentimental urge for personal freedom and the fierce power struggle between them was offset by a nonchalant, *laissez-faire* approach.

It is worthy of note that Uranus transits always coincided with phases in the relationship when John attempted to break free of Yoko's power over him and she actually encouraged him to do so. The most important instance of this centred on their 18-month separation between 1973 and 1974, when Uranus transited over John's Descendant and hit off Yoko's Uranus–Pluto square. But inevitably the compelling mutual fascination characteristic of Pluto cross-aspects eventually resurfaced, preventing a total rupture and drawing them back together again to enact the next chapter of their karmic story.

Right from the start Uranus had stamped itself indelibly on the ballad of John and Yoko, which was to become known to the public as one of the most unconventional love affairs of the century. The almost precise conjunction between Yoko's Uranus and John's Aries Ascendant had injected an explosive excitement into the relationship, John remarking after their first encounter that Yoko was like no one he had ever met and Yoko confessing her belief that John was her soul-mate. And if this were not enough, an opposition aspect between Yoko's Uranus and John's Sun in Libra matched by a complementary square aspect between John's Uranus and Yoko's Sun in Aquarius bonded the couple to one another by an insuperable magnetic force.

Their courting bore all the lunatic characteristics of a typical Uranus love affair, such as Yoko's daily missives to John instructing him to hit a wall with his head and keep laughing for a week or the seven-day bed-in in Amsterdam. Theirs was a nonconformist relationship which turned the standard notion of marriage on its head: they were amongst the first to experiment with the idea of role-swapping, which they pushed to the limits of credibility in a hoax announcement that they had undergone the world's first two-way sex-change operation.

Clearly each accentuated the already well-developed rebel in the other, but more than this the mutual Uranus–Sun contact allowed both to stimulate and expand the other's self-expression and to introduce each other to a new dimension of awareness to which they had not previously been open.

Yoko's Uranus in opposition to John's Sun in Libra symbolized his exploration, through his relationship with her, of a male–female rapport completely different to any he had experienced before. Prior to Yoko, the women in John's life had all been inferior to him in terms of intellect and creative talent. They had been women who had been prepared to acquiesce in his Moon–Pluto desire to control them and had been willing to play the subservient role. Certainly his marriage to the conventional and uncomplicated Cynthia had been a highly traditional affair and their life together had followed the classic pattern of male breadwinner and female child-rearer, except of course that John happened to be a millionaire.

But his relationship with Yoko blasted away all of John's stereotyped preconceptions about women and marriage, inculcated during a standard middle-class upbringing in the charge of his strait-laced Aunt Mimi. In Yoko he had met for the first time with an assertive, independent female with strong opinions of her own, a woman he was unable to dominate intellectually or emotionally and who, unlike Cynthia, had no intention of playing the part of the stay-at-home wife and demanded to be treated as an equal.

Married life with Yoko was to prove to be an entirely different experience to the suburban routine of his years with Cynthia and baby Julian in the stockbroker belt of Weybridge. Suddenly he was catapulted into the bohemian lifestyle of Yoko Ono, avant-garde artist, a lifestyle which lacked any kind of domestic order. Now several days at a time might be whiled away in bed without light of day, making love, making music or getting stoned, a far cry from the regimented pattern of his former family life.

It was not only John's domestic regime that changed under the influence of Yoko's Uranus opposition his Sun. His musical self-expression also entered a new era, turning from the relatively orthodox blandness of Beatle compositions towards a more unfashionable, musically daring style, more obviously in keeping with Yoko's unrepentant individualism and based not on boy-meets-girl love-stories but contentious themes of political and ideological reform.

In Yoko's case it was her fifth house Sun in Aquarius which was to be jolted into new modes of self-expression by the influence of John's aspecting Uranus. Contrary to popular belief Yoko was not nearly as up-to-date as her Aquarian Sun might suggest. Although she was well known for her eccentric artistic stunts, such as her film of 365 bare bottoms, at the time of her meeting with John she had little knowledge of the pop scene, or the Beatles, despite their global renown. By her own admission she was an artistic snob— that is until she met John, who broadened her musical awareness to include an appreciation of rock and roll, firstly inviting her to sit in on recording sessions and later recruiting her as his new musical partner in place of Paul McCartney.

Socially also, Yoko widened her horizons through her relationship with John. Raised in a rich and highly respectable Japanese banking family and having spent much of her adult life mixing with New York high society, she knew little of ordinary, unsophisticated working-class folk, folk like the other three Beatles and many of John's long-time buddies who still formed part of his close entourage when he first met Yoko. It was something of a culture shock for Yoko to find herself in the company of unpretentious and in some cases uncouth Liverpudlians, a development she took some time to adjust to but which eventually enhanced her acceptance of people from all backgrounds.

The problem with Uranus cross-aspects is that just when we are becoming accustomed to being entertained by our partner, he or she is likely to tire of our exclusive company and leave us to our own devices. This was a pattern which duly manifested in John and Yoko's relationship but which they were relatively well equipped to handle by virtue of strong natal freedom urges—Yoko's natal Uranus falling in her seventh house of partnerships and John's natal Venus forming a restless square with his Uranus.

Despite her deep attachment to John and her possible tendency to control him, at times Yoko appeared almost to need to be rid of him, notably on the occasion when she raised no objection to his dating her secretary May Pang, who went on to become John's mistress for the following 12 months or so. John in turn, despite his emotional dependence upon Yoko, refused to be drawn totally into her social circle and would periodically escape to join his rock-and-roll drinking mates in wild, bachelor-style binges.

With six out of ten of her planets in the icy cool signs of Aquarius and Virgo, there is little in Yoko's chart to suggest she had much emotional warmth to offer to John, but this was not what he was accustomed to in women given that both of the two mother-figures in his life had noticeably distanced themselves from him, Julia physically and Mimi emotionally.

What Yoko did have to offer John was her perfect reflection of the contrasting qualities of maternal energy he had been exposed to in his upbringing. Her ability to bring constant excitement into his life coupled with her periodic lapses of interest in him, when she appeared to push him into the arms of another woman just as Julia had off-loaded him as a child onto Mimi, symbolized the combination of stimulation and instability he had experienced in his relationship with his natural mother.

But if at first glance Yoko appeared to have much of the eccentricity of Julia about her, at a deeper level she also exhibited many of Aunt Mimi's steadier characteristics. Like Mimi she could sometimes be possessive of John, may have had a tendency to control him and despite occasional periods of withdrawal, for much of the time was able to provide him with the reassuring structure and discipline he had received in the care of his guardian.

Seemingly a dual embodiment of Julia and Mimi, Yoko could always arouse John's spirit of adventure and desire for danger through the effects of her Uranus conjunct his Aries Ascendant. Yet she could also follow up with the calm, steadying influence he needed to soothe his delicate nervous system by virtue of her Saturn conjunct his Moon in Aquarius, square his Mercury in Scorpio. Yoko's Aquarian Saturn, drawn towards innovation but cautious of total abandonment of reason, could be solidly supportive of John's controversial ideas and outspokenness when necessary, but was always quick to restrain him when he appeared to be going too far.

An excellent buffer for John to bounce his ideas off, Yoko's Saturn could always be counted upon to give him truthful feedback, a rare commodity which John found hard to come by in the wake of his status as a pop idol. Indeed, much of Yoko's initial appeal to John resided in the fact that she never treated him as a Beatle or worshipped at his shrine like Cynthia and most of his other close associates. At a time when John found himself surrounded by the insincere flattery of a host of ingratiating hangers-on, only Yoko could be relied upon to give him the low-down on his mistakes and shortcomings and in this sense she was truly his best friend.

Certainly there must have been times when Yoko's remoteness, tendency to nag or turn a deaf ear as a probable manifestation of her role as Saturn were depressing and frustrating for John, but the

verbal directness of his seventh house Mercury in Scorpio square
Pluto was more than capable of keeping his partner's Saturn in its
place.

A fundamental function of Yoko's Saturn seems to have been to
help channel the emotional explosiveness and verbal violence of
John's Moon–Mercury–Pluto T-square into a more self-analytical
direction. It was at Yoko's suggestion and with her support that in
1970, with a transiting Jupiter–Saturn opposition hitting off the
cross-aspect between Yoko's Saturn and John's T-square, he
embarked upon the then controversial primal scream therapy of
Arthur Janov, in which he regressed into his childhood trauma
with the purpose of obtaining release from the associated pain.

And later on in 1977, with Uranus transiting in conjunction
with his Mercury in Scorpio, he threw himself into an intensive
programme of self-education under Yoko's direction. Unlike John,
who had missed out on much of his schooling due to an inherent
abhorence of authority and establishment values, Yoko was well-
read, having studied philosophy at college. Thrown back on
himself by the intensification of Yoko's business activities at this
time and with only baby Sean for company, John now began
greedily to devour books on all the subjects which had long
interested him but which he had previously neglected, even taking
lessons in Japanese, perhaps in an attempt to prove himself at last
to be the intellectual equal of his Saturn partner.

Overall Yoko appears to have played a mature Saturn role in the
partnership, expressive of her positive karmic attunement to that
planet and reflected in her birth chart by its trine to her
Ascendant, conjunction with her Venus and sextile to her Moon.
This can be compared with John's more abrasive relationship with
Saturn, which falls opposite his Mercury and widely square to his
Moon and Pluto.

John and Yoko's contrasting natal Moon–Saturn contacts are
also apparent in their relationships with their respective mothers.
Despite having raised her daughter with the proverbial Saturnian
rod of iron, Yoko's mother was a stable and reliable figure who
was ever-present in the home. John, however, was confronted
with less acceptable forms of Saturnian energy in the two mother-
figures in his life—firstly in the guise of Julia, unable to shoulder
her responsibilities to him when the going got tough, and secondly
in the figure of Aunt Mimi, who represented Saturn's opposite face

of inflexible allegiance to the status quo.

With such poor Saturn role models it was hardly surprising that John found it difficult to provide Yoko with the steady, uncritical back-up she in turn needed from him. John's Saturn exactly square to Yoko's Venus in Aquarius could be extremely cruel, both in withholding praise and finding fault, Saturn's two prime tactics in undermining his partner's self-confidence when he feels he is under threat. He was especially adept at playing on Yoko's apparent lack of confidence in her desirability as a woman, reflected by her natal Venus–Saturn conjunction, and once publicly castigated her for dressing like a whore when she appeared in a particularly brief pair of hotpants.

By virtue of John's exact natal Saturn–Jupiter conjunction, Yoko's Aquarian Venus also formed a tight square with John's Jupiter, a confusing juxtaposition of his encouragement of her outrageousness and tight-lipped disapproval of her excesses. In this contact with her husband's Saturn–Jupiter conjunction, Yoko was meeting with John's unpredictability, a tendency which also expressed itself in his personality swings between introspective reclusion and self-destructive high living. Adjusting to John's mood changes was undoubtedly a considerable challenge for Yoko, a challenge which she was able to handle only by absorbing herself increasingly in her work.

The importance of the work ethic in the relationship between John and Yoko sings out loud and clear from the chart comparison. With her Neptune conjunct his Venus and his Neptune conjunct her Jupiter, all in Virgo, each admired and aspired towards the other's diligence and efficiency. In fact, work was probably the most important issue in both their lives, centred in John's case around his Venus-inspired music and art and in Yoko's case around her Mars–Jupiter relish for big business enterprise. With little interest in or aptitude for business affairs himself, John marvelled at Yoko's talent for investment, in which she successfully multiplied their already substantial fortune by buying wisely into real estate and dairy farming.

A two-way Neptune contact inevitably throws confusion upon two people's sexual relations with each other, which can encompass self-denial and abstinence on the one hand and insatiable and unbridled lust on the other. In one sense John and Yoko seemed to display an obsession with sex in all of its intricate techniques, suggesting a classic Virgoan fascination with detail and manifest in John's series of erotic lithographs and their 15-minute slow-motion film of his penis in erection. Yet there was also a puzzling element of purity in their relationship, observable in their chaste self-depiction as the 'Two Virgins' on the cover of the album of that name. Clearly John was a highly sensual individual of vast sexual experience, but with Yoko he seemed to regain touch with some of his innocence and freshness, and he felt that their sex-life was on a higher plane than any of his previous physical relationships with women.

More than anything else, two-way Neptune cross-aspects are suggestive of a deeply spiritual love union, the kind in which the two partners are willing to make supreme sacrifices for each other and in which genuine romantic feeling never dies. When Yoko was hospitalized in 1968 with a threatened miscarriage, John touched the hearts of millions by sleeping devotedly at the foot of her bed. And in 1979, almost 10 years exactly after their marriage, the couple still felt sufficiently infatuated with one another to take a full page advertisement in the *New York Times* proclaiming their love for each other and ending with the postscript, 'We noticed that three angels were looking over our shoulders when we wrote this.'

Transits of Pluto to the main cross-aspects between John and Yoko's charts always coincided with important phases of self-development, during which their interaction as a couple was challenged to step up an octave. The 1968 Pluto transit over John's Neptune conjunct Yoko's Jupiter marked one such phase and was responsible for setting in motion John's disillusioned rupture with the Beatles and the beginning of his new creative partnership with Yoko. It was during this transit that, for the first time ever, John openly criticized the work of Paul McCartney, whose musical style was fast diverging from his own and with whom he now had little in common. And it was also during this transit that, to the consternation of long-suffering Beatle fans, he enthusiastically embarked upon the outrageous 'bagism' and 'bedism' stunts inspired by Yoko as part of their campaign for peace.

During this period John's ideology underwent a major transformation, whereby the droll, easy-going and chubby Beatle evolved into John Ono-Lennon, the gaunt-faced and serious-minded political reformer and soul-mate of Yoko. From this time onwards John began to feel himself to be truly at one with Yoko, the woman with whom he publicly unified himself, not only by his official change of name but by a series of published photographs of himself and his wife in which their features are mutually superimposed.

But the most significant of Pluto's transits of the cross-chart contacts was its aspect to John's Sun–Ascendant mid-point and Yoko's Uranus–Pluto square, which dominated 1980, the final year of their life together and an essential tying-up period of karmic issues. Of major importance in John's case was his sailing trip to Bermuda in the summer of that year during which he finally overcame his lifelong fear of the sea, a fear which was undoubtedly associated with its role in stealing his father from him. Compelled to take the helm when the crew fell sick, John was obliged by Pluto's ruthless transformative influence to master his terror of the waves and simultaneously release his long-term resentment towards his father for having 'abandoned' him in favour of his career as a merchant seaman.

In transiting his Aries–Libra Ascendant–Descendant axis, Pluto brought about a new equilibrium between John's combative/conciliatory instincts, a new harmony of spirit which successfully dispelled his nine-year creative block. He wrote two songs during the voyage itself and on landing in Bermuda quickly completed the rest of his final album 'Double Fantasy', to be released just before his murder. With track titles like 'Starting Over', 'Hard Times are Over', 'I'm Moving On' and 'I'm Losing You', was John unconsciously aware of the drastic changes that Pluto was to herald, both in his own existence and that of Yoko?

The thought suggests itself that by 1980 the time was ripe for John and Yoko to release their karmic hold over one another. It may be that the dominant cross-aspect between Yoko's Pluto and John's Sun and Ascendant had become stifling to both of them, yet because of their mutual devotion it was not possible for them to break from one another of their own accord.

For John, in particular, it had become increasingly difficult to envisage an existence without Yoko. Since the birth of his son Sean in 1975 when he had voluntarily assumed the role of house-husband, he had become ever more emotionally and materially dependent upon his wife, who now looked after most of his financial and career affairs. As he sang to Yoko in his last number one hit 'Woman', his life was entirely in her hands, and for his last photo-session with *Rolling Stone* magazine on the very day of his death he chose to be photographed naked and in the foetal position, holding on to Yoko and kissing her.

Could it have been that the spiritual lessons John was intended to learn from Yoko were now complete? Her Pluto square to his Aries Ascendant had been successful in resurrecting the open-hearted, loving side of John, which had taken flight early in his traumatic childhood and had long been masked by his hard and aggressive persona. And in giving John the opportunity to care for his son Sean, Yoko's Pluto square his Sun had enabled him to heal his paternal role—natally John had the Sun exactly quintile Pluto—and to forgive his own father. Finally her steadfast Saturn on his Moon–Pluto opposition had restored his belief in the reliability of women, whom he felt had let him down so badly as a child and whom he had treated with such contempt in his early adulthood.

Yoko's influence had transformed John from a defensive, chauvinistic tough-guy into a gentle, compassionate human being, willing to share his emotions openly on disc. In loving John with all her heart Yoko had accomplished her healing of him. But perhaps the time had arrived for her to begin to work on her own regenerative process, which could be accomplished only by letting John go.

Yoko had recorded a solo track entitled 'Walking on Thin Ice' only a couple of hours before John's death, a title which aptly summed up the sense of risk and uncertainty she was destined to experience as transiting Pluto propelled her towards a new chapter in her life.

In hitting off Yoko's seventh house Uranus square Pluto, transiting Pluto was challenging her to find a new outlet for the powerful creative drive she had formerly lived out mainly through John's achievements. The fact is that despite her fierce independence and desire for equality, her partnership with a genius such as John had inevitably cast her in a supporting role and curtailed her artistic self-expression.

Rather than compete with John's outstanding talent, Yoko had largely confined her activities to the world of big business, an area in which she knew she excelled and in which John posed no competition. Her role had been that of the strong woman behind the successful man, wheeling and dealing behind the scenes to promote John's artistic and financial status, allowing him to concentrate on his music—but at the expense of her own career as an artist.

Now, however, with John's tragic death she was thrown back entirely on her own resources and compelled once again to become her own person. However painful the parting from John, his death obliged Yoko to step out of her husband's shadow and shine once again in her own creative light. For the first time she released an album composed entirely of her own work and in 1986 embarked on a gruelling world tour, not easy for a woman who had always received such bad press.

Despite her Libran dread of loneliness, Yoko came to realize that it was all right after all to be on her own. Yet no sooner had she arrived at this Pluto-inspired insight than a new friend unveiled himself in the figure of Sam Havadtoy, a former business adviser who comforted her after her bereavement and who was destined to bring a new quality of male energy into her life.

It was not only the transit of Pluto which heralded the end of the earthly relationship between John and Yoko. Transiting Uranus was also activating the cross-square between John's natal Uranus and Yoko's natal Sun, indicating that once again John was to challenge Yoko's creative drive to express itself in new, untried ways, but this time without his presence.

Probably the most valuable service that John performed for Yoko during their 12 years or so together was to open doors for her. During his lifetime, in his role as Uranus to Yoko's Sun, John granted her the kind of freedom of lifestyle that only fame and fortune can acquire. As the wife of a fabulously wealthy pop idol, Yoko was able to experiment with her dreams and ambitions on a scale that would not otherwise have been possible for her. And now, through his death, John was paying her the ultimate karmic service of liberating her from her partnership with him to travel along a new independent path.

In moving out of her life John offered Yoko the gift of personal growth, and in this respect he enacted the highest function of Uranus. To many of us also, John Lennon played the role of high ambassador of Uranus in that through his music, his lyrics and his sharing of his emotional pain, he provided us with the opportunity to widen our spiritual horizons.

Acknowledgement: *John Lennon 1940–1980*, by Ray Connolly, published by Fontana.

INDEX

Also in this series . . .

ASTROLOGICAL HEALING
The History and Practice of Astro-Medicine
REINHOLD EBERTIN

Astrological Healing deals with the history and practice of astro-medicine, or 'cosmobiological' medicine. It chronicles astrology's application to healing from the earliest times and also covers Reinhold Ebertin's own invaluable work in this field.

The many links between astrology and alternative medical practices such as homoeopathy and biochemistry are clearly explained and Ebertin provides information about alternative healing techniques used today, how one can work with yin/yang foods for treatment, how cosmic factors play a part in illness and how to calculate a suitable day for surgery. This profound work will be essential reading for all serious student of astrology and the healing arts.

'As always with Ebertin, this invaluable work draws on the whole gamut of his lifetime experience as a practising astrologer/cosmobiologist. It is characteristically clear, direct and practical, showing how we can identify problem areas in the chart and how we can use astrology as an effective tool in the healing process'

— Charles Harvey

Reinhold Ebertin (1901-1988) was one of the very great pioneer researchers, thinkers, innovators and organizers in astrology this century, emphasizing the great importance of social, environmental, educational, cultural and heredity factors in an individual's development. A prolific writer and author, he was also founder of the Ebertin Press and the annual Cosmobiological Research Conferences, and co-founder of the Cosmobiological Academy in Aalen. *Astrological Healing*, his last major work, serves as an enduring tribute to his life.

THE MESSAGE OF ASTROLOGY

The New Vitalism and What It Means for Our Future

PETER ROBERTS

The Message of Astrology seeks to explain by what means the planets can conceivably determine the traits and potentialities with which we are born. Professor Roberts discusses the attitudes of the scientific establishment towards astrology and reviews the considerable body of empirical research into these beliefs, including that of Gauquelin, Elwell and Seymour. He shows how a harmonic interpretation of Gauquelin's statistics leads to the conclusion that there *are* planetary influences that travel at the speed of light.

The Message of Astrology presents a revolutionary theory — The New Vitalism — that accounts for virtually all of the evidence and postulates a separate entity which plans the birth of each individual, both pre-existing and surviving the physical body. It raises important questions regarding the existence of the soul and reincarnation, and has wide-ranging implications for science, philosophy and society.

'A clear and sympathetic account of the evidence for astrology; many astrologers will be pleased to have such intelligent high-level support for their cause. Likewise the uncommitted non-astrologer ought to find this book a clear and fascinating introduction to the area.'
— Charles Harvey

Peter Roberts is an accomplished research scientist. Former head of the Systems Analysis Research Unit in the UK Department of the Environment, he is currently visiting professor in the Department of Systems Science at City University, London. He has had a lifelong interest in astrological research, gaining one of the first diplomas of the Faculty of Astrological Studies, and worked closely with John Addey for many years.

ASTROLOGICAL PSYCHOSYNTHESIS

The Integration of Personality, Love and Intelligence in the Horoscope

BRUNO HUBER

Astrological Psychosynthesis is a holistic approach towards astrology and chart-reading. Based upon the work of Roberto Assagioli, the founder of psychosynthesis, it follows the premise that every human being has a soul, a higher self, which is at the very root of all development processes. The horoscope can be used as a diagnosis instrument to enhance a person's capacity for free will.

In this book Bruno Huber describes the interaction of intelligence, love and personality as a creative function of the whole human being. The three spiritual planets Uranus, Neptune and Pluto indicate one's spiritual development and transformation crises, and a new model, the 'Huber bottle', is put forward to help in understanding the astrological symbolism.

The book is divided into three parts: *Intelligence in the Horoscope* examines the three types of thinking — cardinal (political), fixed (economical) and mutable (social); *Love and Relationships in the Horoscope* explores the social aspect of love, eroticism and sexuality, and demonstrates how to overcome partnership difficulties; and *Personality and Integration* considers the physical, emotional and mental Egos and the development of personality according to the psychological influences of one's surroundings.

Bruno Huber had been a student of physics, astronomy, psychology and philosophy when he turned to astrology in 1947. With his wife Louise he founded the Astrology-Psychology Institute in Zurich, having trained personally for three years under Roberto Assagioli in Florence where he learned to bring psychosynthesis into astrology. The API is now an international concern devoted to teaching and publishing 'Huber Astrology'.

ASTROLOGY ALIVE!

Experiental Astrology, Astrodrama, and the Healing Arts

BARBARA SCHERMER

Astrology is a powerful means of becoming self-aware. Barbara Schermer, whose psychological approach to astrology is strongly influenced by C G Jung, here puts forward an imaginative new way of furthering that understanding. She takes us on a journey through dance, music, art and drama so that the wisdom revealed by astrology is experienced as a living entity — astrology *alive!*

Using a wealth of exercises, rituals, meditations and games, Barbara Schermer breathes life into the planets and signs and teaches astrological principles by experience. Ideal for individual or group work, this book captures the essence of the astrological influences and throws new light on their meaning in our lives.

'In ASTROLOGY ALIVE! *Barbara Schermer does exactly what her title suggests: she brings the astrological chart to life in a way that few other writers have done. It seems destined to become the classic textbook on experiential astrology. It certainly deserves to be.'*
— Howard Sasportas

Barbara Schermer is a pioneer in the development of experiential astrology and an authority on astrological counselling and Kriya Yoga. She also co-ordinates astrology/psychotherapy groups and produces experiential theatre performances.